INCREDIBLE DESTRUCTION IN CENTRAL TEXAS

The Jarrell Tornado

INCREDIBLE DESTRUCTION IN CENTRAL TEXAS

The Jarrell Tornado

Marlene Bradford

Table of Contents

Introduction

Drive down any limited access highway in this country and you will see green exit signs with the name of a community you have never heard of before. Unless you stop for gas or a quick bite to eat, the name will not register in your brain as the signs fly by. For some, the small town is their destination; they are visiting Aunt Mabel for a break from city life. But for most, reading the signs with their unfamiliar names is only a break from the monotony of the drive. We tend to forget that these small communities, often in farming or ranching areas, are home to a breed of people who are fiercely dedicated to their families, their community, and their country. These people have chosen to live where they know everyone three streets away as well as their next-door neighbor. They support their local school, if they are fortunate to have one still, drink coffee and visit with their neighbors at the local café, shop the local stores, and greet each other at church services on Sunday. Outsiders never pay attention to them unless something happens in the area to bring it to the attention of the media---a devastating fire, a murder, or a natural disaster.

I-35 south from Waco to Austin is filled with green exit signs for these small towns: Moody, Hewitt, Lorena, Bruceville, Eddy, Pendleton, Salado, Prairie Dell, Jarrell. I traveled this road hundreds of times and paid little attention to the names until May 27, 1997, when Jarrell burst into the national headlines. A massive F-5 tornado that churned its way through the Double Creek Estates claimed 27 lives in the tightly-knit Williamson County community of some 400. For a few days the country was enthralled with the story as reporters from local and national television stations and the print media descended upon the town to interview survivors and family members of the lost. Many from around the country sent aid to the grieving town, wanting to offer help and support in whatever way they could. But, as is true with so many tragedies, before long the story was forgotten. While a few local journalists wrote additional articles after May of 1997 and Austin television stations ran video clips of the Jarrell tornado periodically, no one wrote a book or even a comprehensive article on the tragedy as the deadlier tornadoes of Moore, Tuscaloosa, and Joplin caught the eye of both writers and readers alike.

In May 1997, I lived in College Station, Texas, where I was completing my doctoral dissertation on the history of this country's tornado forecasting and warning system (published as *Scanning the Skies*). I remember coming home after teaching my noon class that day to find my son watching the television. While I was trying to grab a bite to eat, he yelled that there was a tornado on the ground south of Waco, and the local television station (KCEN: Waco, Temple, Killeen) was following it live. For 6 hours meteorologist Bruce Thomas warned every community that might be impacted by the forming, dissipating, and reforming tornadoes to take cover. At times the twisters were close enough to the station to see them on the television camera that had been pointed out the station's doors. When I heard later that evening that there were fatalities at Jarrell, my heart was broken because I knew that all involved in the warning process from the National Weather Service to the television stations and Jarrell officials had done their part to protect the lives of Central Texans. Citizens, following the meteorologists' instructions or recalling what they had learned about tornado safety, took cover under mattresses in bathrooms and interior closets. Everything went according to script, but the brutal beast bearing down on the town had not read the play.

For days after the tornado, I bought the *Austin American-Statesman* and *Dallas Morning News* and watched the news relentlessly as the story of Jarrell and its loss unfolded. I had hoped someday to write an account of this tragic day, but, as is true with many, I was side-tracked by other projects. While writing the book entitled *Texas Tornadoes: The Lone Star State's Deadliest Twisters*, I came upon my Jarrell file with all of the newspapers and realized that no one had told these people's story. Some of my students at A&M had brought me hand-written, first-person accounts from LaDonna Peterson, Charles Boren, and Allen Meissner, and I knew I could not let them languish in my files. The story of the heartbreak and recovery of this small town which is typical of so many in this country had to be told.

Stories usually have several characters or groups of characters. This one has six: the tornado itself (the weather), the first-responders and rescuers, the survivors, the victims and their families, those who wanted to help in the aftermath, and the community as a whole. All of their stories meld into one that exemplifies the best of the American spirit, the spirit of picking up the pieces and moving on but never forgetting.

As with any major disaster, conflicting reports appeared. The official National Weather Service data base for all severe storms (The National Centers for Environmental Information formerly the National Climatic Data Center) lists all 27 deaths in Jarrell as occurring in a permanent dwelling, but no news accounts include the place of death for Katherine Mayer or Frederick Ripley. The NCDC data base also lists inaccurate ages and genders of some of the victims. Therefore, any errors on my part are unintentional.

Chapter 1

The Tornado's Story

T. S. Elliot said in his poem "Wasteland" that "April is the cruellest month," but in Texas that title belongs to May. More Texans have died in tornadoes in May than in any other month. Seven of the ten deadliest tornadoes in the state's history (Waco, Goliad, Sherman, Frost, Runge, Zephyr, and Saragosa) claimed 442 lives in May. Since 1950, four of the six tornadoes to receive an F-5 rating (including Jarrell) struck during May. Every part of the state is susceptible to these monsters; Central Texas is no exception.

On May 27, 1997, residents of Central Texas were enjoying a warm but quiet morning. School was out for the summer in most towns that dot the map between Waco and Austin. Students were looking forward to a time without school books, a time they could swim or hang out with friends when they weren't catching up on sleep. Workers went to their jobs as usual; farmers tended their crops; ranchers cared for their livestock. In other words, the day began as a routine late spring day, but it would not end in a normal manner.

In Jarrell, an unincorporated town of some 400 located on I-35 about 8 miles north of Georgetown, the morning was warm and humid. Summer was fast approaching, but spring still lingered. The temperature climbed to 79 degrees at sunrise, and a light southerly wind from the Gulf only increased the humidity. The breeze rustled the tall Blackland Prairie grass and gently swayed the mesquite and juniper trees across the rolling hills. Patches of bright orange Indian paintbrushes and white and yellow daisies dotted pastures where cattle grazed, and green leaves marked the rows of beans and corn. A driver along the interstate who took the time to look might describe the scene as idyllic, typical small town America.

At the Storm Prediction Center (SPC) in Norman, Oklahoma, the meteorologists in charge of issuing severe thunderstorm and tornado watches thought this was going to be a routine late spring day in the Great Plains. A low pressure center in Nebraska and the upper level jet stream over northern Oklahoma signaled the possibility of severe weather later in the afternoon in those areas. A weak cold front draped across Texas from the northeast corner of the state to Del Rio on the Rio Grande combined with an ill-defined low-level jet stream meant that the greatest threat in Texas would be strong winds and hail, but the weather pattern was not the typical one that would produce numerous severe thunderstorms or tornadoes. At 1:03 A.M. the SPC issued its outlook for Central Texas: "Moderate risk of severe thunderstorms for hail and damaging winds including Travis and Williamson counties." Weather balloon soundings taken throughout the morning indicated increasing instability in the atmosphere---something was up. At 10:16 the SPC issued a new convective outlook: "Conditions will be favorable for the development of scattered intense storms with very large hail...locally damaging winds and possibly isolated brief tornadoes." It did not appear that the winds were going to cooperate to produce supercell thunderstorm development or a tornado outbreak. But, Mother Nature had other ideas—she didn't follow the rules.

Shortly after noon a thunderstorm developed over southern McLennan County, and at 12:50 the National Weather Service (NWS) office in Fort Worth issued a severe thunderstorm warning for hail from a rapidly developing storm near the town of Woodway. The activity caught the attention of the SPC forecasters. Within minutes (at 12:54) they issued a tornado watch to be in effect until 7 P.M. for much of east Texas and western Louisiana. Williamson County was on the far western edge of the watch which stated: "Tornadoes…hail to 3 ½ inches in diameter…thunderstorm wind gusts to 80 mph…and dangerous lightning are possible in this area." The National Weather Service offices in both Fort Worth and Austin/San Antonio went on high alert. They would be responsible for issuing any severe thunderstorm or tornado warnings in their jurisdictions. The war between nature and man had begun.

Lon Curtis, Bell County Assistant District Attorney and avid storm chaser, had been following the weather situation from his home in Temple 35 miles south of Waco since early morning. Years of experience in researching and analyzing storm data prompted him to keep a close eye on the developing storm potential. While grabbing a quick sandwich for lunch, he noticed a towering cumulus cloud to the north of Temple and stopped to digest the most current data. He returned home, checked the latest television radar, and quickly changed from suit and tie into jeans in preparation for driving into the storm in southern McLennan County only a few miles away. Curtis was heading north across farmland and pastures when he heard a Department of Public Safety dispatcher ask a trooper to check the storm for severe weather development. He decided to check for himself, and as he rounded a curve he saw across the low, rolling hills the first tornado of the day about a mile in front of him. The twister (later designated the F2 Lorena tornado) was exhibiting two odd characteristics: it was moving very slowly, and it moved from northeast to southwest. The great majority of tornadoes in the United States (some estimate that at least 90%) move from southwest to northeast, and their average speed is 30 miles per hour. This supercell was already giving notice that it was not "average," but it lasted only 10 minutes, caused no injuries or deaths, and left behind $75,000 in damages.

Within minutes of the Lorena tornado's emergence from the towering thunderstorm cloud, KCEN-TV, the NBC affiliate in Waco/Temple/Killeen, broke into normal daytime programming to begin what turned out to be a 6-hour marathon. Meteorologist Bruce Thomas followed the developing severe weather and warned the people of McLennan and Bell counties to take precautions to protect themselves and their families. Because very few houses in the area had basements or storm cellars, viewers were urged to go to the lowest interior room of the house, usually a bathroom or a closet, and cover their heads with pillows or blankets. Although they had learned what to do in school, fear and adrenalin take over and often cloud memory and actions. Everyone needed to be reminded that every tornado must be taken seriously—all of these storms   are life-threatening.

Those responsible for saving lives of others, such as first-responders and weather forecasters, must stay on the job during times of imminent danger; they cannot take the time to help their own families. Such was the case of the Thomases. Bruce's wife Ann was eight months pregnant with their second daughter when the first tornado dropped out of the sky near their home in Hewitt just south of Waco. Thomas recalled in an email to the author that "she was taking cover in a bathroom with our one-year-old daughter Betty and our two dogs and cat. Our home was spared that day, but it did make me realize that you truly need more than just a good warning, but a safe place in which to shelter." Unfortunately, later in the day these words would ring all too true.

A supercell, a highly-organized storm with extreme updraft winds that can produce large hail and strong tornadoes, can last for hours. This one was not going away quickly or quietly, and it wasn't following the rules—it kept heading south, paralleling Interstate 35 into Bell County. A sheriff's deputy reported a very brief touchdown at the intersection of Highway 7 and Interstate 35 in the town of Eddy at 1:44. As live pictures flashed across television screens from Waco to College Station (from where I was watching), Bruce Thomas pointed out the tornado virtually right outside the door of the station. Fortunately, the miniscule tornado (only 40 yards wide) dissipated after a journey of 0.2 miles. No damage was reported, but within 2 minutes a stronger tornado (later rated F3) dipped to earth in open fields southeast of Moody and moved into far northern Bell County. In its path, the twister left behind damaged property but again no deaths or injuries. The supercell was still moving slowly southward toward more populated areas of central Texas. If it held together, it could impact the northern Austin suburbs.

Now in Bell County, the severe thunderstorm seemed to say, "I'm not done yet; I'm just warming up." The supercell, still moving slowly south-southwestward, launched another attack with an F3 tornado on the north side of Lake Belton where it destroyed 100 boats and a marina and damaged several lakeshore homes. Almost as an afterthought, the thunderstorm dropped another small, brief F0 tornado from the sky near the Stillhouse Dam in the Lampasas River Valley. Still, no injuries or deaths were reported. KCEN had adequately warned the area to be prepared for the devastation this storm could produce.

As the parent supercell crept southward, the Austin television stations sent reporters to the area of southern Bell and northern Williamson counties to produce live shots of any tornadoes that might develop. They were not disappointed. At 3:07 the thunderstorm produced its sixth tornado about half a mile west of the Prairie Dell exit on I-35. Those traveling the busy highway stopped to observe the beautiful rope-like condensation cloud that appeared to remain stationary in a field for 10 minutes before picking up speed and dancing across fields as it moved southward, virtually paralleling the interstate. The F1 twister damaged trees and several structures but injured no one before it dissipated near the Bell-Williamson County line. This was the warmup for the main event.

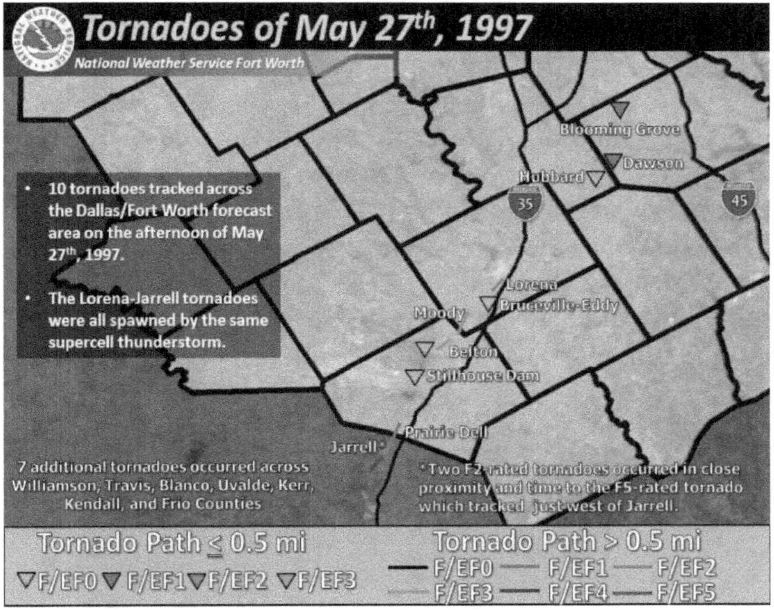

Williamson County was no stranger to tornadoes. Thirty-nine twisters had taken 2 lives and injured 43 since 1950. The most serious one occurred in Jarrell on May 17, 1989, as the town slept. Clocks stopped at 4:02 A.M. when the F3 tornado cut a half-mile wide path through the town, killing 1 and injuring 31. Sharon Thomas died in the debris of her mobile home when the storm lifted it from its foundation and blew pieces in all directions. On the ground for 20 minutes, the winds toppled tractor-trailer trucks on the interstate. Downed power lines and battered vehicles delayed traffic on the highway for hours. In the town, residents aware of the tornado, like Susan Dodson and her family, rode out the fierce storm in their hallways as the howling winds blew debris and scattered belongings as far as 7 miles away. When the storm moved on, Jarrell discovered that 25 houses had been destroyed and 2 schools and 46 mobile homes were damaged. The price tag was $8 million, but perhaps what was even more important for the small town, 50 people lost their jobs at the 18 businesses that suffered severe damage. The community rebuilt, but the terror of that event was still fresh in their minds when storm clouds appeared on the northern horizon in May 1997.

Radar showing Jarrell supercell tornado. From Storm Prediction Center.

When the megastorm crossed into Williamson County, the NWS in Fort Worth transferred responsibility to the Austin/San Antonio NWS office in New Braunfels. At 3:30 this office issued a tornado warning for Williamson County effective until 4:30 P.M. The bulletin that went to law enforcement and television stations said "at 3:25 a tornadic thunderstorm was located about 5 miles west of Jarral (sic) moving southeast at 10 mph. This storm has had a history of producing tornadoes and large hail. The City of Jarrel (sic) is in the path of this storm." Included in the warning were the standard instructions to seek shelter: "Go to the lowest floor of your building. . . cover your head. Stay away from doors and windows. Do not stay in mobile homes or vehicles. . .get into a sturdy building." Austin and Waco television stations blared the warnings to their viewers, and in Jarrell the Volunteer Fire Department activated the warning siren. Simultaneously the SPC issued a new tornado

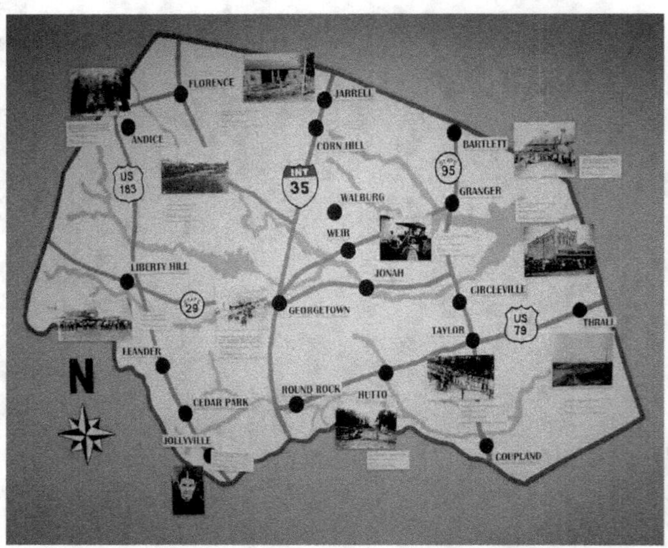

Williamson County map showing location of Jarrell.

watch for south Texas that included Williamson County.

Those who heard the eerie sound knew the possibility of a tornado or at least a severe thunderstorm hitting their town was great. In response, some jumped into vehicles and headed for interstate underpasses or sturdier buildings. Some left mobile homes for permanent houses of friends or relatives. Still others left businesses and hurried home to insure the safety of loved ones. Those who sheltered in houses followed instructions and huddled in bathrooms or closets, often with heads covered with pillows and blankets. As they waited, the storm was gathering strength, ready to hurl itself without mercy on those unfortunate enough to remain in its path.

The small rope tornado that touched down just northwest of Jarrell about 3:40 looked harmless. Maybe this seemingly innocuous storm would bypass the town and move into open country where it would do little damage, but the twister had other ideas. Ted S. Warren, photographer at the Williamson County bureau for the Austin American-Statesman, jumped at the chance to capture shots of the storm. Weaving through traffic as he headed north on I-35, he encountered hail and rain. Near the Jarrell exit he found crowds huddled under the overpass, looking with trepidation at the pitch black sky just north of town. He recalled thinking that he wouldn't find much destruction, maybe only a downed street sign or a barn without a roof. That was before he saw "it," bouncing and dancing its way across the open plain. "It looked like the biggest movie, on the biggest movie screen I had ever seen. For something so destructive, it almost seemed magical to watch."

In just over 1 minute's time, this beautiful, playful cloud that mesmerized those who saw it exploded with fury into an angry, half-mile wide wedge tornado. The swirling black mass had morphed from a minimal F0 tornado into nature's most destructive wind storm, an F5 monster whose winds exceed 260 miles per hour. Some eyewitnesses reported seeing several small funnels before the tornado changed its character. A study of damage patterns after the event suggested that what looked like a single wedge tornado could have been a giant multiple vortex twister. The people of Jarrell didn't care; they knew they were in trouble.

At first the black cloud appeared to be heading toward the main part of Jarrell, a 10-block area that parallels I-35. In the path would be churches, businesses, and the town's schools. But, the rule-breaking tornado seemed to

Tornado approaching Double Creek. From NWS (Ms. Vancil).

change its mind; it veered almost 90 degrees to the west, heading for the uninhabited grassland. It first touched down at Chuck Tonn's farm where it turned structures into kindling and machinery into bales of metal. Next, the twister destroyed the Clawson recycling business and several trailers on the corner of CR 305 and CR 307. Bent steel beams and snapped power poles and trees were witnesses to the storm's destructive power. Slowly edging forward at a measly 5 miles per hour, the indescribable winds blew vehicles through the air as easily as a fall breeze blows dead leaves. Amazingly, the angry storm ripped more than 500 feet of blacktop from CR 305, leaving only a scoured roadbed. If the core of the tornado stayed on its westward path along CR 305, it would bypass or at the worst strike a passing blow at most residences as it headed to open country. At seemingly the last second though, the tornado expanded to a width of three-quarters of a mile and made a slight jog to the southeast which put the Double Creek Estates directly in its path.

The Jarrell tornado barreling down on Double Creek Estates. From Alan Moeller, NWS.

Before the storm Double Creek Estates was a subdivision of 38 modest one-story brick homes built on half-acre to one-acre lots. A few mobile homes dotted the area that was surrounded by small farms and pastures. Some residents had migrated from Georgetown and Austin to escape the hustle of the busier cities and to take advantage of cheaper taxes and a smaller school district. Along Double Creek Drive and Double Creek Spur families lived their lives just as those throughout the country do. They went to work and school, attended church services, and participated in community activities, never dreaming that something so horrible could in an instant end so many of their lives and forever change the lives of those who survived.

The time was 3:48. The Larry Igo home on CR 305 just a few hundred feet east of Double Creek Drive was probably the first inhabited house the storm impacted. As the outer winds peeled shingles from the roof and hurled pieces of debris through fragile glass windows, the family huddled in the safest place in the house they could find, praying the storm would pass quickly. Within seconds stronger winds blew larger chunks of debris against exterior walls and lifted the roof; walls collapsed as they lost their roof support. The incredible winds sheared anchor bolts that had attached the outer walls to the foundation, leaving only vulnerable interior walls. They, too, collapsed within seconds and were blown away. All that remained of the Igo home was the foundation and small piles of rubble. The tornado had claimed its first five lives.

The roaring black cloud, churning slowly like a horrifying movie played in extremely slow motion, next attacked the homes in Double Creek Estates. Just like the Igo house, these homes succumbed to the 260+ miles per hour winds. Roofs disappeared, windows broke, outer walls disintegrated, and interior walls crumbled only to be scattered in all directions by the swirling winds. Unlike most tornadoes that move quickly through a neighborhood though, this unwanted guest remained for minutes at each place which ensured that everything would be pulverized into tiny pieces and blown away. All the homes on Double Creek Drive and Double Creek Spur suffered the same fate. Fatalities occurred at the six houses that were occupied at the time of the storm: Mullins, LaFrance, Carmona, Smith, Gower, and Taylor. But, the tornado was not finished destroying lives. After crossing Double Creek Drive, it edged across open fields toward the Keith Moehring home on CR 396. The house suffered the same fate as the others; four members of the family along with the two Ruiz brothers who had sought shelter in their home perished. After leaving indescribable destruction in the Double Creek area, the twister again altered its course ever so slightly. It moved toward the south-southwest, crossed CR 309, and headed into a heavily wooded area of cedar trees where it dissipated.

Everyone who had seen the tornado described it in different terms. Bud Taylor had one of the more colorful descriptions: "That sky was black as night, just boiling. Like a dad-gum big bull getting ready to charge. Seemed like it set there for 10 minutes making up its mind which way to go." A young survivor said it looked like a giant bear. The size of the monster varied from one observer to another. A man driving away from the storm in his pickup saw a black cloud "hundreds of feet across" in his rear-view mirror. B. J. Barner recalled for the *Dallas Morning News*: "It was huge. It wasn't like a circle funnel, it was like a quarter-mile." Regardless, those who saw the tornado did not care about its actual size or shape; they knew it was dangerous and they had to get away.

Numbers do not do justice to the impact a tornado has on a community, but they do give an indication of the severity of the storm. The Jarrell tornado killed 27 and injured 12. Ordinarily, the number of injured far exceeds the number of fatalities, but this was no usual tornado. Baylor University meteorology professor Don Greene, who studied the Jarrell twister extensively shortly after it occurred, detailed his findings in an Associated Press article in October 1997. He explained that the Jarrell twister which the National Weather Service rated an F5 exhibited several odd behaviors. First, this powerful tornado did not travel far, only about 5 miles; most F5s cover distances of at least 50 miles. Second, the tornado traveled extremely slowly. According to Dr. Greene's study, the Jarrell tornado took 11 to 18 minutes to travel 1 mile through the Double Creek area which translates to about 4 miles per hour; the average speed of a tornado is 30 miles per hour or more. Third, the tornado traveled southwest, the opposite direction of the vast majorities of twisters in the United States. This would help to explain why it moved so slowly. Lastly, Greene concluded that the winds preceding the funnel itself were so strong they blew off the roofs and collapsed the exterior walls which left the residents "exposed to the full force of the tornado."

The Fujita scale ranks tornadoes from F0 (winds from 40 to 72 miles per hour) to F5 (winds that exceed 260 miles per hour). The National Weather Service sends a team of meteorologists and engineers to evaluate every significant tornado to determine its F scale ranking and to uncover any flaws in the warning systems that could be corrected. These men and women are accustomed to seeing the devastating impact strong winds have on structures and lives, but the Jarrell tornado astounded even the experts with its force. The storm cloud had sucked asphalt from roads, bark from trees, and hair from cattle, but even more telling was the lack of debris it left behind. "Instead of the piles of debris that mark the end of most tornadoes, houses simply disappeared, leaving only featureless foundations and bare earth." Perhaps saddest of all of the statements about the severity of the Jarrell tornado came from researchers at the Department of Geosciences at Texas Tech University in Lubbock who explained that those who cannot get out of the way of a tornado as massive and powerful as the one that struck Jarrell have virtually no options. In the words of Dr. Richard Peterson, "In the extreme case when everything can be leveled . . . if you're not in a basement, you're up a creek." This was the sad reality in Jarrell's Double Creek area.

Chapter 2

When the Winds Stopped

Seconds after the winds subsided, Jarrell High School principal John Johnson emerged from one of the school's telephone booths where he had taken refuge to discover that three-foot-long strands of pasture grass from fields nowhere near the school covered his car. That's when he knew something was terribly wrong. Like others in town, he had sought shelter when several minutes earlier the warning siren that sat atop the tower at the fire station blared to notify the community of impending danger. Johnson instinctively knew that his town was injured and perhaps some of his students were hurt.

Just as everyone who saw the monster or survived its wrath had a story to tell, so did each person who rushed to the aid of the small town. Residents of Double Creek who had been away when the tornado hit, hurried to the site to see if they could find loved ones who might have been at home. Law enforcement personnel from Williamson, Bell, and Travis counties as well as volunteer firefighters from several communities dropped what they were doing to rush to Jarrell to help in what they thought would be a normal search and rescue operation.

One of the first on the scene was James Blackmon, police chief and canine officer of Thrall, a small town in the eastern part of Williamson County. As he related the story in 2011 to Blake Hurtik, a journalism student at the University of Texas, one can almost hear his voice crack as he described the horror of that time. He and his deputy knew a storm was coming; they had been listening to the police scanner when the thunderstorm produced tornadoes across Bell County. Before long, they heard about Jarrell, and they knew they had to head to that town to offer what help they could provide. When they reached Round Rock, they found that state troopers had blocked the interstate heading north toward Jarrell. They, along with dozens of other law enforcement officers and troopers, found an alternate route to the stricken town. Riding with Blackmon in an old Plymouth was his canine partner; his deputy followed in the town's police car. As he traveled down CR 305 toward the damage area, the car jolted like it had run off the road. He remembered thinking, "I know Jarrell is poor but this is ridiculous." The road had been paved, but the tornado had ripped away the blacktop as deep as 18 inches. Rescuers had to inch their way through the mud and debris. When he and fellow officers reached the eastern end of what had been Double Creek Estates, they linked arms to form a human chain. Trudging through standing water and mud, they walked forward slowly looking for signs of life, but with only a few exceptions all they found were signs of death.

Blackmon, like other searchers, saw things that deeply disturbed him. He encountered what at first appeared to be a dead animal, only to discover it was the body of a deceased female. He told Hurtik that he still had a hard time talking about it more than 10 years after the fact. "It was real bad. I never saw nothing like that in my life." Most of the bodies would have to be identified through forensics. As Blackmon continued along he observed that "it sandblasted everything." Buildings, livestock, cars, farm equipment, trees, even asphalt looked as though they had been through a blender. Where once houses occupied by families had stood, all that remained were bare slabs and plumbing pipes bent low by the winds. Wooden stakes protruded from telephone poles that the winds had toppled. Barbed wire the tornado had ripped from fence posts entangled bodies of dead cows.

Blackmon remembered that after 8 hours of such horror, he couldn't take it anymore. He returned to his car to let out his dog who only briefly left the vehicle, whimpered, growled, and jumped back in to stay. The canine was not coming out of the car again; he knew the smell of death. When the police chief headed away from the scene of devastation, he offered a ride to others who had reached their breaking point, too. As the old car loaded with 13 officers holding on to the roof, trunk, and hood headed back up CR 305 toward town, they saw in the headlights the terrified faces of residents who could not find their loved ones. In town they passed the fire station which had been set up as a temporary morgue and the church building where people frantically searched for any information on their loved ones. After leaving off his passengers, Blackmon said he took a deep, slow breath and asked "Oh, God. Where is the dignity in this at all? I just can't comprehend this at all."

Captain Shawn Newsom of the Williamson County Sheriff's Department arrived on the scene 20 minutes after the storm left behind its path of destruction. He recalled "I crested over the hill and thought 'This isn't so bad because there's nothing out there.'" As soon as the thought cleared his mind though, he realized there should have been something out there but it was gone. He likened the countryside filled with only solid, flat rubble to films he had seen of the Hiroshima atomic bomb attack. Williamson County EMS Director John Sneed joined Newsom in heading up an immediate search for survivors, but they soon found there were few; the rescue part of the search would be over quickly.

Dennis Jaroszewski, a Williamson County constable, also arrived at what had been the subdivision a short time after the tornado passed. He recalls the horror of seeing a huge machine lift a concrete wall, uncovering the bodies of a woman and her daughter; the child was wrapped in her mother's arms. The constable spoke for many when he told reporters "That's when most of us lost it."

In a personal letter sent to me in the fall of 2000 Allen Meissner recalled vividly that May 27. He had just gotten out of school the previous Friday and was helping his father harvest oats on their farm 5 miles east of Jarrell. Storm reports indicated that the supercell was heading in their direction. As the storm approached, Allen became apprehensive and called his dad on the radio to suggest they park the machines under the shed. His father said to keep cutting because the storm would soon pass, but finally the threatening clouds convinced Mr. Meissner to take his son's advice. As Allen walked to the house, he saw what he described as one of the worst sites possible, a dark funnel cloud that was "slowly creeping across the horizon from north to south." Although he was 5 miles away, Allen swore that, because of its size, the tornado looked less than a mile away and that at any minute it would devour a trailer on their property not far from their house. Allen had always heard it was best not to try to outrun a tornado, but in this case he thought that   the rule was wrong and convinced his dad and sister to jump into their truck and head east toward his grandmother's house in Bartlett. Once inside they turned on the television to watch the weather report; a torrential downpour outside the window blocked any visual sighting of the storm. After the storm had passed, he called his house to see if the answering machine would respond; that would mean their house was spared any major damage. The machine did pick up, but at the same time reports of the Jarrell tornado came across the television screen. Allen and his father headed to their house to check on their equipment; it was fine. They decided they would head to Jarrell to see "what all the fuss was about." When they reached Jarrell, they found confusion. Allen remembered that the law enforcement officers were "driving like mad looking for the damage." The Meissners followed the officers for a while, but finally gave up and turned toward home when they found nothing. It appeared that the weathermen had blown the report of a tornado all out of proportion.

A short while later, someone searching at Jarrell called the Meissner home to ask if they had any large industrial loaders or bulldozers. They said they didn't and asked why they were needed. The voice told them that there was heavy damage at Jarrell; the tornado had struck a neighborhood down in a little valley that was difficult to see from town—Double Creek Estates. The Meissners jumped into their truck and headed to Jarrell to help. As Allen phrased it, "What we saw next, I hope no other person has to ever see." In his own teenage words, he described what so many saw in a way that was real and was not just for media consumption:

"The destruction was unbelievable, for lack of a better word. Where once nice homes use to be, now nothing but dirt. Whole foundations pulled up from the ground and tossed aside. Cows were mangled and mutilated, were scattered everywhere. One of the factors of the storm that caused such gory effects was that the tornado pulled up a couple miles of 6-strand barbed wire fence and sliced and ripped its victims with its force. Right where the tornado started its deadly strike, it took the Tonn's farm equipment, and made a stack out of a cotton stripper, a chisel plow, and a large tractor. The tornado threw this huge machinery around like they were toys. It was almost as if the storm was trying to be funny in the way it just stacked that equipment up on top of each other."

Everyone the media interviewed had a variation on the same words—there was nothing left. Sheriff Deputy R. B. Raby said of the subdivision "It's not there anymore. . . .It's just a flat, vacant field." Max Johnson Jr., son of the pastor of the First Baptist Church, declared "It was like a vacuum sucked everything up." B. J. Barner exclaimed "It's like someone came and just wiped it clean." Governor George W. Bush told reporters after he flew over the devastated area the next day: "It's hard to believe you're looking at a patch of earth where the life was literally sucked out of it."

The sheriff's department blocked access to the area except to those in the search and recovery groups. Angry residents of the Double Creek area were hoping to get to the site of their homes, even if they were no longer there, to recover what might be left of their lives: family keepsakes such as photos, pets who might have survived the onslaught, and everyday items like clothing. Some wanted to check on livestock; others wanted to remove food from freezers before it would spoil. Captain Newsom was adamant that they could not go into the area. They did not know why, but he was protecting them from the horror of finding body parts which were strewn over a large area. Though the site of a demolished home would be traumatic, finding part of a loved one or friend would be unimaginable, an event that would remain in their memory for a long time.

Larry Hausenfluke, superintendent of Jarrell schools, huddled under the I-35 overpass as the tornado swooped down on his town. When it passed, he, like so many others who had seen the twister, ran to see what he could do to help. After a short time at the site, he returned to his office and told his secretary that the school would stay open to serve as a shelter for those who had lost their homes and as a clearing house for any aid that would come to their town. Red Cross workers hurried to Jarrell and set up an emergency shelter at the school. Late into the evening many of those whose homes had been damaged or destroyed drank coffee and ate waffles as they awaited word of what to do next. Julie Thomas, spokesperson for the Austin area Red Cross, was astonished that no one slept on the cots that lined the makeshift shelter that night. Residents who still had a home reached out to their less-fortunate neighbors to provide them

33

with some sense of stability; everyone stayed with family or friends. Dennis Jaroszewski, a part-time security guard at Wal-Mart in Round Rock, contacted the store that afternoon for help with supplies. The megastore responded by giving him anything he needed. He hurriedly grabbed mountains of meat, cheese, and bread to make sandwiches for the rescuers and survivors. At his truck stop along the interstate, Dick Sewell and his staff served people by flashlight for several hours. His business which the tornado eight years earlier had damaged escaped unscathed this time.

Searchers look for survivors in the rubble. From NWS Austin/San Antonio.

When Wednesday dawned bright and dry, more than 150 searchers returned to the disaster site to continue to trudge through standing mud in the hopes they would find a survivor. The previous night the Austin Fire Department had brought in thermal-imagining cameras that could locate people by the body heat they emitted, and police departments brought their dogs that had been trained to sniff out bodies. Occasionally, a call would go out for a body bag—part of a victim had been found and was treated with respect. At midday Thursday the search ended—the toll stood at 27 dead and 27 unaccounted for.

Williamson County Justice of the Peace Jimmy Bitz had the unenviable job of supervising the documentation of the remains. Sheriff Department investigators photographed and catalogued each body before moving it to the temporary morgue at the Jarrell Volunteer Fire Department where Justice of the Peace Judy Hobbs readied the bodies for transport. At 4:30 on Wednesday morning a tractor-trailer truck left Jarrell for the short trip to the new state-of-the-art Travis County Forensic Center in Austin where the medical examiner, Robert Bayardo, and his team would use fingerprints, tattoos, dental records, and any other available method to match the names on the missing list to the remains. Bitz told reporters that the damage the wind and debris had inflicted upon the bodies made identification difficult: "It's just unbelievable what a tornado can do." He would be extra cautious in identifying victims before he filled out death certificates; errors were not acceptable.

In Jarrell families of the missing congregated at the First Baptist Church awaiting the official word of the fate of their loved ones. They hugged each other and cried as Max Johnson Sr., the church's pastor, tried to console those still reeling from the news that not only their homes but perhaps members of their family had been the victims of the horrendous storm. Some brought dental records or photos to aid in identification. Many prayed. Throughout the ordeal they often asked "why," but Rev. Johnson told reporters what he had told the people of Jarrell: "It's too complicated of a question to find an answer." On Main Street volunteers set up a table to ask survivors to put their names on a sign-in sheet to eliminate them from the list of possible dead or missing. Periodically those at the church would leave to check the lists. Although it was obvious to all that many deaths had occurred, the coroner's office would not release the name of any deceased until they were absolutely certain of the identity. The names of the first two confirmed victims of the tornado were not made public until late Wednesday night. Those awaiting word of the others talked among themselves, sharing what information they had on the missing, the safe, and those they presumed were dead.

As searchers continued to comb the Double Creek area, others stepped in to do what they could to help. More donors than the Scott and White Blood Center's mobile unit from Temple could handle arrived to give their blood to the injured. The Salvation Army set up their headquarters at the fire station, and the Southern Baptist Convention set up tables with food and water at the Baptist church. Boy Scouts from Taylor and Granger brought groceries to feed those in need of a meal. One Jarrell couple, Joe and Louise Hoes, had lost their home to the 1989 tornado. Friends and strangers helped them rebuild because they had no insurance. On Wednesday morning they fired up the barbeque pit at their business, Joe's Country Bar-B-Q, and cooked meat to take to the school to feed workers and survivors. They wanted to repay those who had helped them in the way they best knew how. "We will help them as much as we can, 'cause we know what it's like."

Governor George W. Bush came to Jarrell on Wednesday. After an aerial tour of the destruction zone, he shook hands with the people at the school and expressed his condolences for their losses before signing a state disaster declaration for Williamson County. State Insurance Commissioner Elmer Bolton, who was traveling with the governor, estimated between $10 and $20 million in damages. Later the National Climatic Data Center that collects the official storm data for the federal government placed property damages at $40 million and crop damages at $100 thousand. Hard hit were several farms that lost hundreds of head of cattle along with expensive farm machinery.

Not everyone in town was happy with the way officials handled the situation. Especially galling to many was the sheriff department's refusal to let the residents of the area return to check on their property. James Taylor suffered a black eye as deputies wrestled him to the ground when he defied orders to inspect his damaged property. Al Clawson, a tall man with a long beard who reminded some of an Old Testament prophet, addressed the media on Thursday to enlist their support to allow residents to return to their homes and businesses to salvage what they could. Police handcuffed Clawson, and he told reporters that law enforcement "proceeded to whup me with their flashlights" when he resisted. He continued his tirade by saying, "This is our town. We need to be left alone, we need to be able to get to our property and do what we need to do to get on with our lives, thank you very much." Around noon officials declared that the area was open; they believed they had found all traces of missing people.

Those who were so anxious to see what the tornado had left behind were stunned. They soon realized that most of them would need only a few boxes to pack the belongings that were worth saving. Those who had hoped to find important documents, family photos, and other mementos found nothing except "sheets of plastic, knots of sheet metal, pieces of vehicles, miles of twisted fence, snapshots, bills, restaurant checks, a foundation with a water heater and not much else." In most tornadoes residents who dig through piles of twisted lumber, bricks, pipes, insulation, and furniture recover a few reminders of their everyday life but not in Jarrell. Some who thought they had lost everything did recover a pet or a few head of livestock. On Wednesday Georgetown animal control officer Gary Lillo spent hours gathering misplaced pets. He found not only the usual dogs and cats but also four goldfish in a ditch and goats with broken legs. Some of the dogs were placed in temporary pens under a shade tree at the First Baptist Church building. Others, especially those injured, were taken to animal shelters and veterinarians in Georgetown and Round Rock.

Eight farms in the tornado's path suffered loss of livestock, fences, and equipment; some of their homes had been destroyed or heavily damaged. R. D. Hopper, who lived in Huntsville, found only four of his more than 100 head of cattle alive. They had been grazing on land just down the hill from the Tonn's farm. The tornado had killed the others outright, even piling a dozen against a piece of farm equipment, or injured them so severely they had to be put down.

For days the media roamed throughout Jarrell looking for the best human interest stories they could find. Newspapers from small towns and big cities from New York to Los Angeles and all of the major television networks sent reporters. When reporters and camera crews saw the disaster site, a somberness set in. Captain Newsom recalled that one radio reporter who had no camera just walked around looking for someone to interview. Newsom told him he was too busy to talk to him, but the reporter responded: "Please give me an interview. There's nothing I can say that will describe this." His statement seemed to be the theme for several days. Even hardened veterans found it difficult to control their emotions when they heard the stories of the families who suffered so much. For nearly a week CNN had a broadcast team in Jarrell, and the major networks (NBC, CBS, and ABC) devoted segments of their nightly news casts to the town. It seemed as though everyone in America was fascinated with the story of the tiny town that had lost so much.

Chapter 3

The Survivors

Each survivor had a unique story to tell the media. A very small number had survived their houses blowing apart around them. Many had left their homes to take shelter away from the tornado's path when they saw it approaching their town. Some were fortunate enough to have been away from home when the tornado barreled through their neighborhood. Most in Jarrell, however, had not suffered physical damage to themselves or their property, but they had endured the emotional trauma of seeing friends and families struggle through their losses.

The Donnie Peterson family began their morning as usual on May 27. As he headed out the door for work, his wife LaDonna urged him to be careful and to have a great day. Almost as an afterthought she added that she hoped a storm would blow through and take the heat and humidity away; at 5:30 the heaviness of the air and the heat were already oppressive. Little did she realize how prophetic her words would be.

LaDonna and her seven-year-old son Duston decided to take an early swim. They knew that by afternoon the heat would be too intense to be outdoors. Shortly before 1:00 the Storm Prediction Center issued a tornado watch for Williamson County until 7 P.M., but Mrs. Peterson was unaware of the potential danger. She did not want the distraction of television while she paid bills, but about 2:30 Duston turned on the television in the living room and then returned to his room. Noticing the television was still on, LaDonna randomly flipped through the channels and heard a special weather report. A tornado had touched down north of Temple. Within minutes the meteorologist confirmed another tornado had damaged structures on Lake Belton. LaDonna called her father who lived in the area, and he reported that they were all safe but the storm was moving in her direction. While LaDonna continued to monitor the weather on television, she had mixed feelings. She was not worried because the sky showed no evidence of an approaching storm, yet for some unexplained reason she was very uneasy. As she continued to listen to storm reports and warnings, clouds moved in from the north and the sky became overcast. Peterson did not think a tornado would strike Jarrell, but should the weather situation deteriorate she wanted her mother-in-law who lived next door to be aware of the situation. Juannita Peterson's line was busy, but within seconds LaDonna's phone rang; her mother-in-law had been trying to call her. The two women discussed what to do, and LaDonna said she might come over later. Within a few minutes, however, LaDonna told Duston to get his shoes and clothes on because they were going to his grandmother's for a while "just in case." They grabbed their poodle Chocolate, and LaDonna picked up the papers she had been working on and headed to "maw's."

When she and Duston arrived at her in-law's home, LaDonna found her sister-in-law Bonnie Hammett and daughter Bonita were there. Kermit and Juannita Peterson's home was a substantially-built one on County Road 396 a short distance west of Double Creek Drive. Juannita was on the phone, and Bonita was watching television when suddenly the warning sirens sounded. LaDonna rushed to the front porch and saw a "big black cloud about one mile away that stretched from the sky to the ground." Frantically she ran into the house and hollered for everyone to get into the bathroom. She put the children into the bathtub and covered them with cushions she had grabbed from the couch, and the adults squeezed in because they thought it was the safest room in the house.

The storm did not strike immediately, but the family knew it was still there because of the pressure they felt. Anxious to see what was happening, LaDonna left the bathroom to peak out the front but saw nothing; however, when she looked out a side window, she saw a frightening sight—the tornado was stripping chunks of blacktop from the road and hurling debris everywhere. She hurried back to the shelter of the bathroom. Through the window she saw the tornado rip the roof from the barn and the donkey fly by. Suddenly, the bathroom door blew open, and LaDonna covered her head with a cushion. To keep the children calm the family all held hands and sang "Jesus Loves Me" and "Old McDonald." As the storm loomed ever nearer, LaDonna prayed "please God please don't take my family." Wood, rocks, hay, dirt, and everything imaginable pelted the group in the bathroom, but no one was hurt. When rain began to fall, they realized the tornado had passed. As they move toward the door opening, they saw a pile of furniture blocking their exit. LaDonna and Bonnie climbed over the pile, and the others left through the bathroom window. As rain soaked them, the Peterson family realized how lucky they were. The exterior walls and roof were gone, and everything except the bathroom was a shambles. LaDonna looked toward her house, but it wasn't there. Neither were any of the houses on Double Creek Drive. She later told reporters that "it was like a bomb had been dropped on us." Her mother-in-law took the children to the neighbors while LaDonna went to look for those who might be hurt. Like many of those who survived, she was in shock. Her first thought was "It looks like a war zone out here." She found a little girl and her mother and stayed with them until paramedics arrived then she walked toward her own house. As LaDonna approached, she saw that her home, travel trailer, pool, and everything were gone. Only broken remnants of her family's life filled the yard.

LaDonna's next thoughts centered on getting medicine and food for her family. She called the pharmacy for prescription refills and headed to Georgetown with her son, niece, and sister-in-law to get the medicine and something to eat. While at the pharmacy, LaDonna realized that they must look "like someone that lives on the streets. We're dirty (covered in mud) and we stink." She used the restroom to clean up Duston as much as possible so he could eat. At that point she felt so inadequate because for the first time she could not provide a bath, clean clothes, and a bed for her child. LaDonna realized that all of those who had survived the tornado in the Peterson's bathroom were homeless and lacked even the basic necessities of life.

LaDonna, her husband Donnie, and Duston spent that night with their oldest daughter's family, and early the next morning they headed to Jarrell to see what they could recover from their property, but authorities told them they could not enter. LaDonna recalled that "for the next 48 hours we went through so many emotions: grief, fear, anger, hurt, and humiliation due to the fact of being bombarded by the media and law enforcement. Not only had we experienced the storm and survived but now everyone wanted control over us." When they were allowed to return to their property at the end of the week, they found only a few things they could keep.

The Peterson home showing the bathroom where the family survived. From NOAA.

A short distance down CR 396 Virginia Davidson was mowing her lawn when she saw the tornado heading directly toward her home. She hurried into the house and huddled under a blanket in her bathtub. As the howling winds blew the house apart, they lifted her and the tub into the air and tossed them several hundred feet. "I was hanging there in the air, and all I could see was pitch black." When Virginia landed, she still had the blanket with her. Her husband James rushed home from his job in Austin to find his house destroyed and his wife missing. As he searched through the debris, he feared the worst. "I was looking for her body. I didn't expect to find her alive; not when you saw what I saw." He didn't even recognize where he was. The winds had sucked all of the fence posts out of the ground; property lines were not evident. Then, he saw a woman, bleeding and covered in mud, walking down the road toward him. It was Virginia. He took her to the hospital where they treated her only injury, a gash to her leg.

Not far from the Davidson house, Wayne and Polly Gibbs had built their home on a rise at the end of a private road that paralleled Double Creek Drive. From their porch they could see the Double Creek subdivision. As the Gibbses sat in the dark that Tuesday night and watched workers pore through the rubble of their neighbors' homes, they felt sad that their home was heavily damaged but thankful that their family was safe. Polly's two daughters who were visiting at the time of the tornado survived when the winds demolished portions of the residence. It was the family's second close call—the 1989 Jarrell tornado destroyed another daughter's house.

As the tornado bore down on their home on Double Creek Drive, Billy La France hurried his wife Debby and 10-year-old daughter Kristin into the bathtub. He crouched nearby on the floor; the tub wasn't big enough for all of them. They covered their heads with couch cushions. Debby recalled "I could hear things start to hit the house, tinkling sounds, it sounded like the roof was tearing off, things were tearing apart. And that's the last thing I can remember." Searchers found Debby in the branches of a peach tree near the ruins of the modest home. Her daughter Kristin lay in the mud nearby, bleeding but alive. "I think this tree is what saved us, saved me and my daughter because I was in the tree and she was on the ground near it," Debby told an interviewer. She thought that if the tree had not been there, "we would have been blown on where my husband was taken and he was taken three houses down the road and he was killed."

Emma Mullins lived next door to the La France's home on Double Creek Drive. Early in the afternoon on the day of the tornado she left work at the L&M Café in Georgetown to check on her two step-grandsons, 5-year-old Ryan Fillmore and his 13-year-old brother John Reyes, who were home alone. A few weeks before, Emma had taken in her son Paul and his family until they could get back on their feet. Just like the other houses on the fateful road, the Mullins house succumbed to the onslaught of the extreme tornado winds. John was the only one to survive. Rescuers took him to Georgetown Hospital where confused relatives finally located him and tried to piece together the fate of the rest of his family. He told relatives from his hospital bed that he blacked out when the tornado sucked him into the air, but he remembered seeing a board pierce his grandmother and Ryan flying from the home. When he awoke, he could see that only the slab foundation remained. His cousin told reporters "it looks like that poor boy got into a car crash or that someone beat him up real bad. He's got stitches on all different parts of his body." Doctors told remaining family members that he would not suffer permanent physical injuries, but the emotional scars would be a different matter.

The 1989 Jarrell tornado had destroyed Gabriel Hernandez's mobile home as he and his pregnant wife cowered under their bed. When he built a new home at 115 Double Creek Drive, Gabriel dug a 7-by-9 foot underground cellar to use in the event another tornado hit the area. While Gabriel was at work on Tuesday, his wife and their three children took advantage of his foresight. They survived unscathed as the most destructive part of the tornado roared overhead, obliterating any sign that a house had once stood there. Although they were trapped for half an hour because piles of debris covered the cellar door, the Hernandezes were glad to be alive; most of their neighbors were not as fortunate. When reporters asked about his shelter, Hernandez responded: "A lot of people say that I'm the most intelligent guy in the whole neighborhood. But I think I was the most frightened. That's what saved my family."

While some survived the onslaught in their home, others chose to flee when the black cloud threatened their safety. Diane Howell and Charlie Boren, who had both worked overnight shifts, had settled in for a day's sleep in their home near the intersection of CR 305 and CR 307, only a short distance from Double Creek Drive. Charlie related to me in a letter that Diane had a hair appointment that afternoon. As she was closing the gate, her 12-year-old neighbor, Charles Bates, told her there were tornadoes on the ground near Belton, about 40 miles north of Jarrell. Diane returned to the house and told Charlie about the tornadoes. He turned on the Weather Channel to monitor the situation, and she drove to a hair appointment. As she approached I-35, Diane saw a small tornado in her rearview mirror. After watching it for a few minutes, she determined it was headed for her house. About the time Charlie realized the weather situation was serious, Diane burst into the house shouting frantically "Get up! Get up! Get your clothes! Don't put them on! It's here! It's here! There's a tornado right outside headed this way!" While Diane scooped up the dog, Charlie grabbed his clothes and headed for the door where he saw the monster. He knew that they had to make a split-second decision about what to do; there would be no second chance if they chose wrongly. If Diane had not left the car doors open and the motor running, they might not have escaped to safety. Charlie ran barefooted over the gravel drive, clinging to his clothes, and hopped into the car. He described the twisting cloud closing in on them as a monster that "looked like a huge pillar, with a halo around the top, holding up the sky." About half way between their driveway and CR 307, their escape route, they saw a car fly around the corner. A pair of frantic eyes peered out of the windshield. Larry Igo was heading home to warn his wife and three children. Charlie waved for him to turn around but to no avail.

Diane headed south on the county road, away from the tornado. She urged Charlie to take a picture, but Charlie kept telling her "Just drive! Hurry up!" They, like many others that day, took shelter under the I-35 overpass. Charlie thought it was not a very good refuge, but it might save the car from hail damage. Under the bridge they heard what "sounded like many jet aircraft warming their engines before takeoff." Curiosity overcame Charlie, and he climbed the hill to the access road overlooking the valley they had just fled. A huge cloud bank, unrecognizable as a tornado, enveloped their subdivision. What appeared to be thousands of white birds circled inside the swirling cloud mass. In an instant Charlie knew those were pieces of vinyl siding from their home. As he started to return to the underpass, freezing air rushed up the hillside where he stood, and a strong wind carrying everything imaginable blew over his head. He returned to the overpass as the rain, blown horizontally by the wind, began. Just as suddenly as it had begun, the rain stopped. Everyone who had been under the bridge was cold, wet, and shaken by the event, but they were all alive.

When the Department of Public Safety released traffic, Diane and Charlie headed home. Charlie described what he saw. "We could not tell where our house had been! Everything was so disorienting! It was a mud flat!" They backed up to the corner and counted four driveway culverts. Charlie recognized a fence post and a pile of debris across the yard where a telephone pole had been. "Yep, this was it!" As he walked around the spot where their house had once stood, he encountered a bull that was impaled on the phone pole. In a state of shock Charlie started "acting like we were actors in a movie and this wasn't real." Diane thought his actions were very inappropriate, but he later explained that he was trying to protect her.

Tracy Arnold watched as the twister got bigger. Inside the family-built rock-walled home near the Double Creek Estates, she prepared for the worst as she, her two children, and a niece and nephew huddled together in a closet waiting for the onslaught of the winds. Keith Bukowsky had also seen the tornado as he frantically raced his dump truck toward the house where his sister-in-law was trying to protect the children from the storm. As he pulled into the yard, the tornado was only about a thousand feet away. He screamed for everyone to get out of the house and into a car. They sped to the underpass where they watched helplessly as the tornado churned slowly along the road where their house stood. After the storm passed, they returned to find the entire house, including the closet, was gone. Arnold credited her brother-in-law with saving their lives. Bukowsky told reporters: "They say you're not supposed to run from a tornado, but I think we did the right thing."

Tonya Wagers was watching a soap opera at her home on Double Creek Drive when she looked out the window and saw the funnel. She saw the thin, narrow cloud hit the ground and spawn two other tornadoes. Not waiting to see if it would hit her house, Tonya fled in her truck. When she came back to the site where her house had once stood, all she could find was a cage for the dog. She and her husband had survived, but her house, a van, three trucks, and five dogs were gone. So, too, were many of her neighbors on that unfortunate street.

Lynette Tonn and her son Ronnie drove away from their farm just minutes before the tornado arrived. The storm blew the roof off their one-story home and uprooted numerous trees before moving up a slight hill toward the three-bedroom home where Lynette's other son, Chuck, lived. Fortunately, he was at work in the U.S. Soil Conservation Service office in Belton; the twister left nothing but a pile of rubble behind. The ferocious winds carried a check from his house 35-miles to San Gabriel where a woman working in her garden found it.

Randy Denson and eight others were sitting in his cousin's doublewide as the storm approached Jarrell. When the storm got too close for comfort, the group decided to try to outrun the twister. They jumped into two pickups and took off down the road. Denson recalled one of the men hollered, "Grab the beer and let's go." He didn't know how fast he was driving, but he could see it in his rearview mirror. The group was lucky---the tornado destroyed the doublewide.

Gail Beaver was painting a house in the targeted subdivision when he decided to stop for a nap in his recreational vehicle parked nearby. When he went to sleep, the sky was cloudless, but when he woke up, conditions had changed drastically. Fearing the storm would wreak havoc on his unstable home, he put his children into the car and hurried for a highway underpass where they escaped injury. Similarly, Robin Frey and her 7-year-old son watched from an underpass as the monster roared not far from their shelter.

Patrick Tucker was tired after just moving into his mother's home on CR 305 in Jarrell. After breakfast on that sunny Tuesday morning, he and his mother Kay talked briefly with neighbors in their Double Creek Estates subdivision before Patrick headed for his job in Austin. When reports of tornadoes in Jarrell came across the television, Patrick hopped in his truck and battled hurricane-force winds and driving rain as he sped northward along I-35. A police blockade at the entrance to the subdivision stopped him. When he demanded access to the area to see for himself whether his mother and her home had survived the tornado, police again refused. Nearly hysterical from fear, he bypassed the police and jumped a barbed wire fence. What he found was nothing. "I found a neighborhood that was as if it never existed. It was just razed. There wasn't even a slab to my mother's house. Everything was gone. Absolutely zero." Thinking his mother was dead, Patrick went to the high school gym that was serving as a shelter. There in a crowd of sobbing storm victims he spotted red hair like his. Tears streamed down his face when he realized that his mother was alive. She had gone to a dentist appointment and had decided not to drive home when she heard the tornado warning.

Vicky Nunn and her young son had lived in one of the two houses on Double Creek Spur. Fortunately, they were not at home at the time the tornado struck. According to her she couldn't even figure out where her house was. "It's just dirt there. Everything is gone."

Whether they survived in their home like the Petersons, under a bridge as Diana Howell and Charles Boren, driving away like Randy Denson and his friends, or being away from home like Kay Tucker, all would agree with LaDonna Peterson who said "we were luckier than some and not as lucky as others, but we thank God every day to be here."

Chapter 4

Remembered with Love

Twenty-seven is just a number to most people, but to the residents of Jarrell who experienced the horrors of the tornado it represents the number of large cracks in their hearts that will never be filled. Too often we think collectively of the victims of disasters, whether natural or man-made, but each fatality leaves a gaping hole in the lives of those relatives, friends, and communities left behind.

All deaths are sad, but the untimely death of a child seems to bring even more grief than usual. While the town lost about 7% of its population, the Jarrell monster claimed a disproportionate number of young lives. Fourteen of the victims were school-age (5 to 17). In addition to this gloomy fact, nine families lost two or more members. One family of five and another family of four perished together on that tragic day in May.

The healing process began in earnest on the Saturday following the tornado when many of Jarrell's heartbroken survivors trekked from one funeral to another to say goodbye to friends and family who had borne the full brunt of the deadly tornado. The three services on Saturday were held in Georgetown to accommodate the large crowds of mourners. In coming days other funerals and memorial services would take place in the Central Texas area or, in a few cases, out of state.

Vicki Taylor and Jonathan Kehl

Pastor Joe Knight of the Georgetown Church of the Nazarene conducted the first funeral of the day for Vicki

Taylor (age 36) and her son Jonathan Kehl (16). As with all victims, the caskets were closed. Nearly 300 viewed a photo display of the mother and son taken during their participation in church activities. Vicki had been instrumental in building the congregation after she moved to the area from Colorado Springs seven years earlier. Large pictures of Mrs. Taylor and Jonathan, which would later be given to family members, adorned the tops of their caskets. The pastor's sermon emphasized their love for the Lord and other people and included a poem by Michelle MacDonald, one of Jonathan's cousins. She summed up what happened to many that horrible day in Jarrell: "They both did not have a chance to say goodbye. They died in terror, but they died together, in each other's arms. I know they are with God now."

Struggling to survive as a single mother, her church community was thrilled when Vicki bought a nice three-bedroom home for her family in Double Creek Estates a few years earlier. She worked as a home health provider, and on the day of the tornado Vicki was home in bed with a knee injury. Jonathan, who had just completed ninth grade at Jarrell High School where he played football, was scheduled to begin his first job at Albertson's the day following his death. In love with the Lord, Jonathan hoped to enter the Nazarene Bible College in Colorado Springs to become a preacher. Pastor Knight praised Jonathan saying "The dominant feature of his life was his heart for people." Mother and son were buried in Colorado Springs.

Larry, Joan, Audrey, John, and Paul Igo

When the tornado sirens sounded, Larry Igo (age 46) shoved John and Paul, his 15-year-old twin sons who had been working with him at his vintage car restoration shop, into the car and barreled toward home to be with the rest of the family. His wife Joan (47) and daughter Audrey (17) reached their modest home on CR 305 in the Double Creek subdivision about the same time. Audrey had been helping her mother at Jarrell Elementary School where Joan was a special education teacher. As the family followed instructions to get away from windows and seek a small room in which to protect themselves, the once-distant dull roar exploded into a more ominous howl. Although the Igos, like the other families in their neighborhood, followed tornado safety instructions, they could not know that this tornado was unique and didn't follow the rules. As the incredible winds reached their home, the roof blew off and the walls collapsed leaving the family vulnerable to the mercy of the storm. Sadly, the Igo family all perished as their house, the first one struck in the Double Creek Estates, vanished. Perhaps even sadder was the fact that the tornado did not touch either the school or the auto shop; they had all rushed home into danger.

The Igos had moved to Jarrell from Austin when their children were small and became thoroughly enmeshed in the community's activities. The entire family whom First Baptist Church pastor Max Johnson jokingly called the Von Trapp family (from the "Sound of Music") were an integral part of the music at the worship services. Larry served as the music director, Joan played the organ, Audrey played piano, and the twins sang in the choir. Joan frequently led in community activities. Audrey who would have been a senior in the fall made plans to attend the University of North Texas where she could perfect her music talents. Her brothers were active on all of the local sports teams and worked at the Jarrell Market.

Five caskets topped with pictures and flowers filled the front of the First Baptist Church in Georgetown, the home congregation of Larry Igo's parents. Nearly 1000 people crowded into the building to show their support for the remaining family and to mourn with fellow townspeople. Throughout the crowd sniffles blended with six of the Igo's favorite songs. Especially touching was a solo that Larry's sister, Linda Cobb, managed to sing through her tears. She knew how vital music was to her brother, so important that Larry would lead every verse of every song during services. In Larry's honor John Warden, pastor of Grace Baptist Church in Salado, led every verse of "Amazing Grace" and "Victory in Jesus" along with other Igo family favorites. Pastor Max Johnson noted that although they had many reasons to be sad, they also had reason to be grateful for the way the country had responded to the tragedy. Throughout the service he stressed that the gathering was a celebration of life, not a recognition of death.

After the service ended, those who grieved, many with tears still glistening in their eyes, watched with heavy hearts as the pallbearers carried the caskets to the five hearses waiting to take the Igo family to the Independent Order of Odd Fellows (I.O.O.F) Cemetery in Georgetown. The only sound heard was the rustling of leaves in the gentle breeze, a much different wind than had blown through Jarrell only four days earlier.

Cindy, Brandi, and Stacy Smith

As more than 350 friends and family of the Smith family entered the Gabriel Funeral Chapel in Georgetown, they saw three caskets, each adorned with a large portrait and flowers. The chapel was packed, and an overflow crowd filled the lobby, listening to the proceedings through speakers. This final funeral of the somber Saturday, like the ones before it, celebrated the lives of multiple family members who perished together the previous Tuesday. Max Johnson, pastor of the First Baptist Church in Jarrell where the Smiths were active members, and Joey Wilson, leader of the youth group at Riverbend Church in Austin, both emphasized that they were a loving family. The Smith family, like many other victims of the tornado, were laid to rest in the I.O.O.F Cemetery in Georgetown.

Cindy Smith (age 36) who had grown up in Jarrell was the office manager at the Jarrell cotton gin. She doted on her girls and followed her daughters to all of their activities. Thirteen-year-old Brandi was a gifted student who had just completed the seventh grade. Her 1010 on the practice SAT led many to believe she would have been the class valedictorian. Only the Sunday before her death she had discussed the meaning of Memorial Day with her church youth group, saying "the best thing about America is the freedom to be who you want to be." Her ability to speak had earned her awards in the University Interscholastic League speech contest. As is true of many teenagers, Brandi loved to shop. A classmate revealed that "she was a mall freak." Brandi's ten-year-old sister Stacy, who had just completed fifth grade, loved animals and sports, especially softball and basketball.

Keith, Cindy, Erik, and Ryan Moehring

When Keith Moehring (age 40), a Blue Bell Ice Cream route man, heard about tornadoes in the Jarrell vicinity, he rushed home to his home on CR 396, only a short distance from Double Creek Drive, to join his wife Cindy (40) and his sons, sixteen-year-old Erik and fifteen-year-old Ryan. The family stood in their front yard watching the storm approach. By the time they realized the monster had turned directly toward them, it was too late to do anything except run into the house and take what shelter they could find. Witnesses told Keith's father, Red Moehring, that the storm appeared to just stand over Keith's house, exerting a force great enough to pull clothing off the family members. Red realized that "there's no way they ever could have thought of surviving for a second in that thing."

Keith was an Air Force veteran who had worked with his father in a Georgetown bakery before joining Blue Bell. An avid fisherman, he had great success in local bass tournaments. He also coached youth baseball and operated the chains at Jarrell's football games. His wife Cindy had recently started a housecleaning business. Ironically, that Tuesday afternoon she had called two of her many clients to warn them about the storm. Erik had been working at the HEB in Georgetown about eight months. Co-workers said that although he was quiet and somewhat timid, he was "a real hard-working kid", "an all-American kid." His younger brother Ryan was just the opposite—popular, funny, and sometimes outspoken. When he wasn't playing football or basketball, Ryan enjoyed video games. Red described his family as "just plain folks who wouldn't stand out in a crowd, but they were the backbone of society. They're just good people."

Red Moehring had the unenviable task of telling his wife who was recovering from a stroke that their family was gone. When a positive identification was made early Thursday morning, he sat beside her bed and said, "Honey, I got to tell you something: our kids didn't make it." Immediately she began to cry. In a somber segment of "Fatal Twisters: A Season of Fury," Mr. Moehring told the reporter: "You cannot say why me? Why my family? Because there's no answer. If you have loved ones, tell them you love them because they might not be here tomorrow."

One week after the tornado, services for the entire family were held at Gabriel's Funeral Chapel in Georgetown. They were buried side-by-side in the I.O.O.F Cemetery in Georgetown.

Maria, John, and Michael Ruiz

The 1989 tornado that struck Jarrell moved the Ruiz's mobile home on CR 307 off its slab. Taking a lesson from that day, the Ruiz brothers, John (age 15) and Michael Ruiz (14), fled their home for the safety of a sturdier neighbor's house, the Moehring home less than half a mile from theirs. The exact details of their deaths remain unclear. The boys may have died on route to the Moehring's, although the National Weather Service data that lists place of death for all tornado fatalities said that all 27 deaths in Jarrell were in permanent structures. The death of Maria Ruiz (50) is even less clear. Some accounts say the tornado engulfed her car as she was on the way to find her sons, but if all of the Ruiz family had reached the Moehring home, they perished along with their host family.

Earlier that day the brothers, who loved basketball, rushed to the high school gym after breakfast to shoot hoops. The high school athletic director described them as "just real good kids, good athletes; they like to compete and be involved." Michael, in particular, had a great sense of humor and loved to make people laugh. Their mother Maria (50) worked as a licensed vocational nurse for Wesleyan Nursing Home in Georgetown. Wesleyan co-workers described her as "the nicest sweetest person there was," and said that many of the residents she cared for were grieving at her death. An extensive search of the literature revealed nothing about the funerals or burial of the Ruiz family.

Ruth, Michael, and Satyn Carmona

The Carmona's lived at 114 Double Creek Drive. Like many of their neighbors that day, they huddled hopelessly in their home as the onslaught of the winds peeled the walls away. Ruth (age 34) was a stay-at-home mother who spent a great amount of her time trying to keep up with all of her athletic children's sporting events. Thirteen-year-old Satyn played softball, basketball, and volleyball and ran track. Although around adults she was shy, her friends called her sweet, funny, and friendly. Satyn's brother, Michael (15), was a serious student who played numerous sports, especially basketball. The family was interred in Calvary Cemetery in Omaha, Nebraska.

Bernice and Brian Gower

When dark clouds began to fill the sky on Tuesday, Bernice Gower (age 37) stopped in downtown Jarrell to help her mother, Sylvia Gaswint, move merchandise into her small resale shop before winds and rain could damage it. Then, she hurried to her home on Double Creek Drive to be with her son Brian (11). Bernice, a special education teacher at Cedar Valley Elementary School in Killeen, looked forward to spending the summer at home with Brian. In the fall Brian, a Cub Scout who loved Power Rangers and playing video games, would be in sixth grade at the same school. Like so many that terrible afternoon, mother and son died in their home. Bernice's sister-in-law knew "they had died in each other's arms; they were always so close." That closeness extended to their church activities at Great Hills Baptist Church in Austin where both sang in the choir.

When the storm subsided, Mrs. Gaswint jumped into her car and followed emergency vehicles streaming toward her daughter's neighborhood. Looking toward the spot where the home should have been, Sylvia "couldn't see a single house." Throughout the night the family that included Brian's father Gerald held out hope that Bernice and Brian had survived. At the church building that served as the information center for those hoping to hear good news Mr. Gower showed pictures of Brian whose birthday had been the preceding month. With a foreboding in his heart and choking back tears, Gerald recalled that Brian couldn't blow out all of the candles on his cake. He also remembered that the last night Brian had spent with him, his son had watched several storm chaser videos since "he was interested in tornadoes because he remembered the one in 1989." All Mr. Gower could do was wait and pray, but those who returned from the scene of devastation held out little hope to the families of those still missing. When the word of the death of their loved ones came, the family made arrangements for a funeral on Saturday morning, but a misidentification of one of the deceased ended those plans. Mother and son are buried side by side at the Berry Creek Cemetery in Georgetown.

Emma Mullins and Ryan Fillmore

A few weeks before the tornado Emma Mullins (age 44) had taken in her son Paul, daughter-in-law Linda, and their two children to help them get back on their feet. The good-natured head waitress at L&M Café in Georgetown had opened that morning at 5 A.M., welcoming the usual customers and inquiring about those she hadn't seen in a while. When she heard of potential bad weather, Emma left the café about 1:00 to check on her grandsons who were at her home on the corner of Double Creek Drive and CR 305. Like others on her block, she, Ryan (5) and John (13) took shelter when they saw the monster approaching, and, just as most of her neighbors who were at home that day, she perished. Ryan also died in the wind's onslaught, but John survived.

Jarrell neighbors and café customers remembered Emma as a charitable, caring person. Eddie White, a café regular, told reporters that "she was known to call elderly people at home if they didn't show up for coffee just to see if they were OK. She would bring them food if they needed it." After the 1989 Jarrell tornado, Mrs. Mullins was one of the first to volunteer to help her neighbors by doing laundry, cooking food, and whatever else she saw to do. Sadly, it would be her remaining family who would need help and comfort from neighbors this time. Emma and Ryan are buried together in the I.O.O.F Cemetery in Georgetown.

Billy LaFrance

Next door to the Mullins home, Billy LaFrance (age 41) and his wife Debbie and daughter Kristin watched in horror as the monster cloud approached their home. They followed conventional advice and headed for the bathroom where Debbie and Kristin huddled in the bathtub and covered their heads with cushions. Lack of room left Billy sitting on the floor next to the tub, holding on with all his strength. Their house, like those of their neighbors, could not withstand the incredible wins. As the walls blew away, the winds picked up the family like ragdolls and flung them away from where their house had once stood. Debbie and Kristin survived, but Billy's body was found three houses away. Two other children, Aimee, Jarrell High's salutatorian, and Joshua were not at home at the time of the storm.

Mr. LaFrance, an employee of an electronics company, loved to fish and watch the Dallas Cowboys. He is buried in Cook-Walden Capital Parks Cemetery in Pflugerville.

Katherine Parish Mayer

An extensive search of public records and publications revealed no details about the circumstances of the death or the funeral of Katherine Louise Parish Mayer. Williamson County death records did confirm that she died in the Jarrell tornado. Thirty-year old Katherine Mayer and baby Justin are buried in the Cedar Grove Cemetery in Trinity County, Texas.

Frederick Ripley

An extensive search of public records and publications revealed no details about the exact place of death and funeral of Frederick Jeremiah Ripley. Williamson County death records did confirm that he died in the Jarrell tornado. I was unable to find the final resting place of Frederick Ripley (age 22), although Social Security death records confirmed he was born on May 15, 1975, in the state of California.

I have studied tornadoes for more than 25 years, and I still consider the Jarrell one the saddest for two reasons: (1) the number of children who lost their lives, and (2) the number of victims who would not have died if they had stayed where had been before rushing home. In no way am I blaming any of the victims, especially the adults who did all they could do to protect the children. It's human nature to protect your family, and the people who lived in the Double Creek subdivision did just that, protected themselves and their families as they had been taught to do. I am sure that every adult who lives in tornado-prone areas has heard the warning to seek shelter in the most interior part of the lowest level of a building. For homes without basements this is a bathroom or an interior closet. Fearing the children might not know this, parents and grandparents hurried from places of safety into harm's way in an attempt to protect their loved ones. All of the Igo family were in buildings that were spared the tornado's wrath (Joan and Audrey were at the school and Larry and the twins were at his business), but they wanted to be sure the other family members were safe. The same is true of Keith Moehring, Emma Mullins, Bernice Gower, and Maria Ruiz who each rushed home from places of safety to protect their children. Sadly, the Ruiz brothers died doing what they had been told to do: get out of a mobile home and seek shelter in a permanent structure. None of them could have known that this tornado was extraordinary and didn't play by the rules. Those caught above ground in this twister's path had little chance of survival.

Houses in Double Creek where deaths occurred. House 1 is
Mullins; 2 is LaFrance; 3 is Carmona; 4 is Gower; 5 is Smith; 6
is Taylor; 7 is Igo; 8 if Moehring. Williamson County Appraisal
District map modified by author.

Chapter 5

Days and Years after the Storm

Something in the American character compels us to help those who are in need, especially those who suffer a natural disaster such as a flood or storm. Even if we can't put our "boots on the ground," we reach out to our fellow countrymen through charitable organizations. For days after the tornado, our country seemed to hold the people of Jarrell especially close to their hearts and responded with physical and emotional aid.

Food and water for first responders and searchers is essential in the first hours and days after a disaster. Large businesses such as Walmart and H.E.B. donated food and other necessities, including work gloves, masks, and lights, almost immediately. Small businesses and individuals did what they could to feed the workers. Joe's Country Bar-B-Q cooked meat to take to the school to feed workers and survivors. Although she had no friends or family in Jarrell, Bertie Gandy of Temple brought pots of baked beans, collard greens, potatoes and homemade cornbread to supplement the standard sandwiches. She told the *Austin-American Statesman* that "we figured they'd only have sandwiches and such to eat and I thought they'd want something more." This attitude was prevalent throughout the coming days.

Large disaster relief organizations, such as the Red Cross and Salvation Army, hurried to Jarrell to set up kitchens, provide shelter, and assist in any way they could. The Red Cross set up a shelter for those the storm had displaced, but no one used it; they all went home with friends and neighbors. The Texas Baptist Men, an organization that sends workers to disasters around the globe, set up their two mobile kitchens at the First Baptist Church to feed not only victims and rescue workers but also the media. On Wednesday morning following the storm they provided breakfast for more than 600. More than a dozen volunteer organizations set up in the small town to do whatever was necessary to help those impacted by the tragedy cope. The need was great. According to Gary Warmink, a representative of the Aid Association for Lutherans branch in Georgetown, 77 families lost everything from homes and cars to heavy farm equipment.

Within hours of the story of the Jarrell tornado reaching the ears of the American public, people from areas outside central Texas began to collect clothes, food, and household items for the survivors. Tractor trailers filled with donations from around the state as well as Oklahoma and New Mexico arrived at the Jarrell High School gym which served as the relief center. Volunteers worked diligently around the clock to stack the boxes filled with everything from food to diapers and cleaning supplies. Mounds of clothes filled the bleachers. So much arrived that Stephanie Spencer of Jarrell who was serving as a volunteer told the press, "We can't possibly use it all...Please don't send us more goods. We have too many as it is. What we really need is money." The public heard the plea, and money began to pour in.

Early Thursday morning in Austin, television station KVUE joined with the Salvation Army, the Red Cross, the Capital Area Food Bank, and radio stations KVET and KASE to set up a one-stop site at the Auditorium Shores where the public could donate food and money. One young man gave his $5 weekly allowance, and hundreds dropped off personal checks that ranged from $20 to $1000. Organizer Thad Rosenfeld told the *American-Statesman*, "Israeli bus tokens, we take it all." One woman summed up the feelings of many of those who contributed: "This is my way of saying I'm grateful it didn't happen to me."

Concerned employees of many of the corporations with a presence in Austin and the surrounding area urged their employers to give. Dell Webb Corporation, a land development company in Georgetown, donated $5000 to the Jarrell Relief Fund and raised $20,000 for the Red Cross. Randalls Food Markets donated 1 percent of the purchases made on their store card to the fund. Motorola donated $15,000. Some companies such as Advanced Micro Devices agreed to match employees' donations, and others organized future events. The outpouring of support was so great, the United Way/Capital Area asked the 100 largest companies in Central Texas to hold off on contributions until they could better assess the needs of the stricken community. Professional athletes pitched in as well. Golfers on the Celebrity Players Tour that was playing at Prestonwood Country Club in Dallas the weekend following the tornado announced they would contribute $50,000, and former Dallas Cowboy Bill Bates donated a hefty $150,000.

Churches, as usual, were quick to respond to help those in need. Virtually every size congregation throughout the state called upon its members to help fellow Texans in need. The Aid Association for Lutherans (AAL), headquartered in Appleton, Wisconsin, stepped in with a $6000 check for Jarrell, and AAL branches throughout Texas held bake sales and coffees to help out their fellow Texans. The bishop of the Dallas Area United Methodist Church called on all local congregations to take up special contributions for Jarrell, and the conference sent $2000 to help. One congregation, the College Street Church of Christ in Waxahachie, did not forget the huge debt the impacted farm families faced in replacing livestock and equipment. The minister, Walter Buchanan, personally handed the Tonn family a check for $5000 and gave an additional $5000 to the other tornado victims.

Money and physical goods were not the only things donated in the first days. At the fire station volunteers assembled a lost and found for small family mementos that volunteers brought in. These volunteers from many areas around Jarrell as well as the town itself filled large cardboard boxes with children's toys, books, and jackets found in the fields. Other boxes held pieces of a family's life: birthday party photos, pieces from favorite games, even cancelled checks. One man from Austin found plastic farm animals and a child's teddy bear when combing the barren fields. Although he would never know if the child to whom the toys belonged survived, he, like so many of the volunteers, felt that they just had to do something to help.

Housing for many was a critical need. The Red Cross and Salvation Army issued vouchers for a month's rent, and the Salvation Army worked to get mobile homes donated for families to use while rebuilding their homes. As they did in so many areas hit by disasters before Jarrell, Amish and Mennonites carpenters from as far away as Wisconsin brought their skills and materials to build new homes for the displaced. From June through November the Mennonite Christian Aid Ministry sent 405 volunteers from 15 states to help Jarrell rebuild. Most used their own personal or vacation time and paid their own way to Texas while Jarrell citizens provided food and housing.

In August 1997 volunteers from the Lutheran brotherhood in Williamson County, Riverbend Church in Austin, and St. David's in Austin appeared in Jarrell to undertake a multi-home rebuilding project. The Cement and Concrete Promotion Council of Texas provided the materials and the blueprints for new residences for four families that lacked insurance to rebuild: the Tschoerner family, Vicki Nunn family, Paul and Linda Mullins family, and Debby LaFrance family. These buildings were constructed of concrete-filled polystyrene blocks. From the inside these homes looked like any other, but they could withstand winds up to 200 miles per hour.

Memorials serve two purposes: aid in the healing process and remind those in the future about lives that were lost or events that occurred. Such was true in Jarrell. One year after the tornado, survivors, preachers, and volunteers dedicated a pink granite memorial near the town fire station with the names of all who had perished in the May 1997 tornado as well as the name of the 1989 tornado victim. In 2002 the town built a larger memorial on the Igo property which the family donated to honor their relatives. The Jarrell Memorial Park, built on the site of the Igo home, houses a community center, playgrounds, picnic areas, and ball fields. Around the building are twenty-seven trees, one for each life lost, that serve as a reminder of the devastation of the terrible day in May. Nearby two community storm cellars serve as reminders of Jarrell's past, and an outdoor warning siren soars into the air over the fields where the Igo house once stood.

Pink granite memorial near fire station. Author's photo.

Close-up of names on monument. Author's photos.

Jarrell Memorial Park showing trees planted to honor
those lost in the tornado. Author's photo.

Memorial plaque in Jarrell Memorial Park honoring Igo
family. From City of Jarrell.

Community storm shelters in Jarrell Memorial Park.
Author's photo.

Throughout the summer students at Jarrell High School struggled to come to terms with the loss of so many of their friends. When school resumed in the fall, feelings of sadness still remained. At a memorial roll call on the first day of school, students answered "Present in our memory" when the names of the deceased were called.

The football team decided to dedicate its season to their fallen teammates: John and Michael Ruiz, Ryan and Erik Moehring, and John and Paul Igo. Although they might falter in adding numbers to their wins column (the team had not had a winning season since 1986), the Jarrell Cougars were going to "play every game for them." School officials and parents worried that a losing season might add to the grief the players felt, but the team was determined to follow through. The first game of the season on that hot September night was against the favored Bruceville-Eddy Eagles. What sounded good in the locker room, however, was not translating into playing on the field. Late in the second quarter Jarrell trailed 18-0. After the half-time break, the Cougars came roaring back like their mascot. They managed to score 4 touchdowns while holding the Eagles to only 6 more points. When Chris Arldt looked at the scoreboard and realized that the final score was 27-24 in their favor, he told *People Weekly* that a powerful feeling came over him. He realized that their 27 points represented the 27 lives lost in May. The Cougars went on to win 2 more games before suffering a defeat. One mother of a football player expressed the feelings of many when she said "The town has suffered loss, and this is something good." In spite of the losses, a sense of accomplishment and togetherness filled the minds of the football players and boosted the spirits of one man in particular, Juan Ruiz. While Juan was at work, his entire family (wife Maria and sons John and Michael) perished in the tornado. Matt Kitchens approached the grieving father and told him that he and his teammates would "play their hearts out in the memory of his sons." At first Ruiz thought that attending the game would be too painful, but he was glad he decided to go. After the game he related that "I felt good." He, like so many others in the stands, gained a sense of solace in watching the team play in remembrance of their friends who were no longer able to run out onto the field.

A few years after the tornado, Jarrell built three new schools, each designed to withstand any tornado that might stalk the town in the future. In 2013 Superintendent Bill Chapman explained to Joel Thomas of the Dallas CBS station that all of the schools had concrete-reinforced safe rooms. Classrooms were built in two circles with doors facing into a common hallway. The rooms in the interior circle, built to storm shelter specifications, had no windows and walls of reinforced concrete. Should the need arise, all of the children and staff could comfortably fit into the inside "safe" classrooms without having to go outside. Windows in the other rooms in the schools had a protective glaze that makes it safer if broken or a film to prevent shattering. As a constant reminder of what can happen, the Jarrell ISD Administration Building has a memorial wall on which hang plaques dedicated to the twelve students and one teacher who died in the 1997 tornado.

The first Thanksgiving after the tornado was especially hard for Jarrell. Many family members who would have been gathered around tables were absent. The Thursday before Thanksgiving, the town held a pot-luck supper. Victims and volunteers joined together and exchanged thank yous and paused for a moment of silence in remembrance of happier Thanksgivings in the past. Debbie LaFrance, who earlier in the month had moved into her new house on the same lot where the old one had stood, spoke for many when she said "the holidays are going to be hard."

Rebuilding had begun, but many empty concrete slabs and temporary housing mixed with the newly-constructed homes in the Double Creek area. There were signs of returning to some-type of normalcy, though. The Petersons and Hammets had rebuilt their homes on the acreage they had lived on before the storm. Two days before Thanksgiving fourth graders from a nearby school district planted a tree on each piece of property that the twister had impacted. Someone noticed that a tiny rosebush that Cindy Moehring tended on their property had four blooms, one for each member of the family that was lost. Although this day should have been one of thankfulness for the ones who survived, everything was not well. Squabbles over the division of money set neighbor against neighbor. Dianne and Steve Johns had begun a fund with $50 to aid the 80 families who had lost so much. Little did they realize that donations from around the country would flood into the fund which reached $1.3 million. So much fighting over the distribution of the money ensued that the Texas Attorney General's office intervened, but this was the exception to the rule. Most were glad that friends, neighbors, and even those from afar who knew no one in the area came to their aid.

In the years since 1997 Jarrell has changed. New schools have been built, and new houses have blossomed across the landscape. In 2001 the community incorporated, and a new water tower looms as a symbol of growth and progress. Some people have moved away, but others stayed and rebuilt, some on the site of their devastated home. Even Double Creek Drive appears somewhat as it did on that day in May before the big monster descended upon the unsuspecting residents. On the tenth anniversary of May 27, 1997, former city councilwoman Ruth Dotson told the *Temple Daily Telegram* that Jarrell was growing, "but it's still a local town. We want to keep it that way, even as the town continues to grow. And we want the people who lost loved ones that day to know that they're not forgotten, and they never will be."

A few years after the tornado, a view of Double Creek Drive. Author's photo.

Jarrell rebuilt.

Chapter 6

Was the Jarrell Tornado Really an F5?

"She is the most beautiful woman in the world." "Butter pecan is the best flavor of ice cream." "I think this is the best movie this year." Every day we hear someone making a statement of judgment. The same, to some extent, is true of rating tornadoes. If a building can be completely blown away by a 150-mph wind, how do we know the storm didn't pack a wind of 250 mph? On what do we base our conclusions? To help standardize tornado wind speed assumptions, meteorologists use a scale based on the destruction the twister left behind.

In 1970 Japanese scientist Theodore Fujita working at the University of Chicago devised a tornado rating scale that used structural damage to estimate wind speeds within the tornado itself (see table below). Since 1971 the National Weather Service has assessed every reported tornado and assigned a Fujita or F-scale rating based on the single most intense example of damage in its path.

Fujita Tornado Damage Scale

SCALE	WIND ESTIMATE *** (MPH)	TYPICAL DAMAGE

F0	< 73	**Light damage.** Some damage to chimneys; branches broken off trees; shallow-rooted trees pushed over; sign boards damaged.
F1		**Moderate damage.** Peels surface off roofs; mobile homes pushed off foundations or overturned; moving autos blown off roads.
F2	113-157	**Considerable damage.** Roofs torn off frame houses; mobile homes demolished; boxcars overturned; large trees snapped or uprooted; light-object missiles generated; cars lifted off ground.
F3	158-206	**Severe damage.** Roofs and some walls torn off well-constructed houses; trains overturned; most trees in forest uprooted; heavy cars lifted off the ground and thrown.

F4	207-260	**Devastating damage.** Well-constructed houses leveled; structures with weak foundations blown away some distance; cars thrown and large missiles generated.
F5	261-318	**Incredible damage.** Strong frame houses leveled off foundations and swept away; automobile-sized missiles fly through the air in excess of 100 meters (109 yds); trees debarked; incredible phenomena will occur.

Over the years, meteorologists and engineers who study tornado damage found that the Fujita Scale was lacking in certain areas: (1) it was too subjective because it was based only on the damage the tornado left behind and did not take into account the differences in building construction and (2) the rating was based on the worst damage in the tornado's path, even if it was only one structure. The most obvious flaw was the scale's inability to absolutely assign a wind speed based on the collapse of a house. If a structure blew away at 190 mph could you reasonably argue that the wind speed was 250 mph? What if the tornado hit no buildings or only weak structures like mobile homes? As a result, controversies often swirled around rating a tornado at F-5. Such was the case with the Jarrell tornado. The description of both an F4 and F5 tornado reasonably fit the 1997 Jarrell storm, but some even suggested an F3 rating.

Initially, the NWS rated the Jarrell tornado an F4, but on Wednesday following the tornado, Al Druemond, the manager of the Austin/San Antonio NWS forecast office, reclassified the Jarrell tornado as an F-5. Fellow NWS meteorologist Bruce Thoren, who also surveyed the damage, said than an F-5 strips the bark off trees and obliterates houses down to their slabs. The men estimated wind speeds peaked between 260 and 270 mph, but were most likely in the 270-mph range. One difficulty with rating the Jarrell twister was the lack of piles of debris that most tornadoes leave behind. Houses had simply disappeared leaving only concrete slab foundations, a few plumbing pipes protruding from the ground, and bare earth. Shingles, wood, bricks, furniture, appliances, and all vestiges of life a home would contain had seemingly been ground into tiny pieces. The monster had debarked trees and even sucked asphalt from roads, which led those looking at the path of destruction to conclude the Jarrell tornado had been in the "incredible damage" category.

Asphalt peeled from road. From NOAA.

Only the slab is left. From NWS.

Moehring home before and after. From KVUE.

Not everyone agreed that the Jarrell tornado deserved an F-5 rating. Tim Marshall, a structural engineer and meteorologist who is perhaps the country's preeminent rater of tornadoes, studied in detail the construction of the homes that were destroyed in Jarrell to determine the lowest wind speed at which the structures would fail. In an article in *Stormtrack* magazine Marshall thought that the slow movement of the tornado, which could have taken from 3 to 5 minutes to pass a given home in the subdivision, was a significant factor in the shredding "like in a blender" of the homes, regardless of how they were constructed. He concluded that the lowest winds in the Jarrell tornado were "around 200 mph, or upper F-3. Note that F-5 winds (greater than 260 mph) would have caused the same devastation too." In other words, he didn't know for sure. On the twentieth anniversary of the tornado, Marshall didn't give the tornado a rating but modified his opinion about its ferocity. He told reporters for KVUE that "I have never seen that intensity tornado damage in my career. Houses were obliterated. I'm talking about everything in the house was taken. The destruction was so intense it serves as a baseline for which other tornadoes are rated against." He concluded that "Jarrell was not really survivable above ground."

A few days after the tornado the Office of the Federal Coordinator for Meteorological Services and Supporting Research conducted both a ground and aerial survey of the areas the Jarrell tornado impacted. Two members of the team, a structural engineer at the National Institute of Standards and Technology and a meteorologist from the NWS in Alabaster, Alabama, issued a report in July 1998. They concluded that "the worst wind damage can be explained by wind speeds corresponding to an F3 rating," and "an F4 rating or the F5 rating officially issued by the NWS need not be assumed to explain the damage." Researchers from Texas Tech estimated the winds at or below 200 mph which corresponds to F3.

A blogger on the Extreme Planet website disagrees with these conclusions. He based his conclusion on destruction other than homes. "More pavement was removed in Williamson County than in any tornado in history, and the ground scouring was perhaps the most intense ever surveyed over a large area. The telephone poles in the worst affected areas were snapped a few feet above the ground – an indication of extremely violent wind acceleration. Cars and heavy wreckers were ripped apart and granulated into small pieces, and many were never found. Video of the tornado also shows extremely violent rotation comparable to other F5 tornadoes. The tornado quite literally left no damage indicators with which to judge higher winds. It is undoubtable, however, that the tornado deserved the F5 rating it was awarded."

Why is there such a discrepancy in rating tornadoes? The Storm Prediction Center's "Frequently Asked Questions about Tornadoes" has a good explanation about rating them:

"F-scale winds are derived from engineering guidelines but still are only judgmental estimates. Because:

1. Nobody knows the "true" wind speeds at ground level in most tornadoes, and

2. The amount of wind needed to do similar-looking damage can vary greatly, even from block to block or building to building; therefore, damage rating is (at best) an exercise in educated guessing. Even experienced damage-survey meteorologists and wind engineers can and often do disagree among themselves on a tornado's strength."

An even better question might be, what difference does a tornado rating make? My opinion, reached after studying tornadoes for nearly 30 years, is the "wow factor." According to the Storm Prediction Center, only 59 tornadoes since 1950 have received an F5 or EF5 (an expanded tornado rating system that went into effect in 2007) rating. That is elite company when one considers from 1950 through 2017 there have been more than 71,000 tornadoes in the United States. An F-5 rating gets attention from the media, researchers, and (I'll admit) historians.

Regardless of the rating of the Jarrell tornado, all who study the ferocious storm can agree that the devastation was some of the worst seen in modern history (since 1950). They can also agree that no rating system can lessen the heartbreak a community suffers.

Chapter 7

Tornado Safety

Tornadoes are scary. Even professional tornado researchers and chasers recognize that the unpredictability of these storms make them extremely dangerous. A pencil-thin tornado can explode into a mile-wide wedge monster in a minute. More frightening may be their unexpected change in direction. People who were not in their path may suddenly find the ferocious winds assaulting them. What should someone who sees a tornado in the vicinity do? Two things: (1) assume all tornadoes are deadly, and (2) get out of its way.

TORNADO SAFETY TIPS

1. **Assume every tornado is a deadly one**. Avoid staying in its path, if possible. If it isn't possible to avoid the tornado, have a place to take shelter.

2. Learn the difference between a tornado **watch** (tornado *could happen* somewhere during the time of the watch) and a tornado **warning** (a tornado *has been sighted* in your area—take the necessary precautions to protect yourself and others). Whenever a watch is issued for your area, be sure you have a way to keep up with the weather. Phone apps from television stations and various weather entities are available which will notify you in case of a tornado warning in your area. Some cities such as where I live have a reverse 911 call service to notify residents, even in the middle of the night. If possible, have a weather alert radio, especially if you live in a mobile home or in an area susceptible to night time tornadoes.

3. At home put as many walls between you and the outside as possible. This is usually a downstairs bathroom or closet, but be sure the room does not have a window or an outside wall. If your house has a basement, take shelter there. In a 2-story home a good place is often a storage area under the stairs. I always told my students that if they had time to put on sturdy rubber-soled shoes (if your house is hit, there will be broken glass and maybe downed electric wires), to be sure they had their cell phone in their pocket, and to grab something such as a pillow, chair cushion, blanket, or even a bicycle or football helmet to cover their head. The old myth of opening windows should be ignored. Don't waste time—the first thing the winds will do is open them for you.

4. **Mobile homes are especially vulnerable to high winds**. Anyone who lives in a mobile home, whether it is tied down or not, needs to leave and seek shelter in a sturdy building. If your mobile home park has a community shelter, go there.

5. At school, follow the instructions of the principal or person in charge.

6. Ask if your workplace has a designated safe area. If not and you are in a multi-story building, the stairwell is a good place as are inside bathrooms, but stay away from windows and get downstairs as much as possible.

7. Many malls have designated tornado or safety shelter. Look for them if severe weather is a possibility on your shopping day.

8. In restaurants, grocery stores, or convenience stores walk-in coolers or refrigerators are the best places to go; bathrooms are also a possibility, but be sure they don't have windows.

9. **Cars are not a safe place to stay in a tornado**. If you are in a car and see a tornado approaching, leave your car and take shelter in a sturdy building. If you are out in the country and no building is available, get into a ditch or a culvert. Be sure to get away from your car. There are cases

of people being killed by their car rolling on top of them. DO NOT GET UNDER A HIGHWAY BRIDGE OR OVERPASS—they act as wind tunnels. If you are traveling on the highway, be sure you know what county you are in should the weather turn severe. Tornado warnings are usually issued by county.

10. If you find yourself in the open when a tornado is approaching, try to get to a building. If none is available, find a low place such as a ditch and get as flat to **where you would take shelter and, most importantly, keep informed about the weather.** the ground as possible.

11. **No matter where you are, when a tornado watch is issued, think about**

IF A TORNADO WARNING IS GIVEN FOR YOUR AREA, REMEMBER "SPIN"

S---shoes; be sure you are wearing closed toe, rubber soled shoes

P---phone; have your cell phone in your pocket so you can call for help if needed

I---identification; stick your driver's license in your pocket; you might need it to get into your home if your neighborhood is blocked off

N--news: have a ready source of information such as a NOAA weather radio, local TV station, or cell phone app

Appendix A

Williamson County Tornadoes 1950-2017

Date	Time	F scale	deaths	injuries
5/21/2011	800 pm	0	0	0
4/27/2009	315 am	1	0	0
4/27/2009	310 am	1	0	0
5/14/2006	250 pm	0	0	0
11/23/2004	608 pm	0	0	0
11/23/2004	1105 am	0	0	0
11/23/2004	1051 am	0	0	0
11/23/2004	1040 am	0	0	0
11/15/2001	450 pm	0	0	0
3/16/2000	420 pm	0	0	0
3/16/2000	412 pm	2	0	0
3/16/2000	408 pm	0	0	0
7/4/1998	1200 pm	1	0	0
5/27/1997	305 pm	3	0	15
5/27/1997	**240 pm**	**5**	**27**	**12**
5/27/1997	235 pm	2	0	0
5/27/1997	225 pm	2	0	0
5/13/1994	1205 pm	0	0	0
6/1/1992	733 pm	0	0	0
4/28/1991	145 pm	0	0	0

5/17/1989	302 am	3	1	28
12/10/1985	440 pm	2	0	2
12/10/1985	152 pm	1	0	1
09/19/1983	107 pm	0	0	0
6/4/1983	930 pm	1	0	0
5/18/1983	1115 am	1	0	0
4/20/1982	1230 pm	1	0	0
5/16/1981	1225 am	1	0	4
2/10/1981	113 am	2	0	0
8/10/1980	225 pm	0	0	0
4/7/1980	448 pm	3	1	5
2/29/1980	815 pm	1	0	0
7/28/1978	215 pm	2	0	0
4/14/1977	520 pm	2	0	0
5/7/1975	500 pm	1	0	0
10/30/1974	700 pm	2	0	0
10/21/1972	730 pm	1	0	0
5/24/1972	345 pm	1	0	0
5/24/1972	322 pm	1	0	0
5/24/1972	322 pm	1	0	0
4/27/1972	556 pm	0	0	0
11/17/1971	330 pm	2	0	0
4/8/1968	400 pm	0	0	0
09/4/1967	735 pm	0	0	0
5/18/1966	330 pm	1	0	0
5/18/1966	330 pm	2	0	0
5/18/1966	330 pm	1	0	0
5/18/1966	330 pm	1	0	0
4/26/1964	600 am	2	0	0

3/10/1963	1000 pm	1	0	0
6/29/1961	525 pm	1	0	0
5/2/1958	350 pm	1	0	0
4/24/1957	220 pm	3	0	1
4/24/1957	145 pm	1	0	0
09/4/1956	400 pm	2	0	0
6/5/1955	418 pm	1	0	0
4/30/1954	610 am	3	0	6

From NWS San Antonio Database

Appendix B

Description of Jarrell Tornado from

Storm Events Database

Several eyewitnesses reported that the Jarrell tornado was preceded for a period of 8 to 10 minutes by a series of short-lived very small tornadoes that formed from the same supercell thunderstorm. These touched down, then dissipated in order.

The first tornado in Williamson County formed near 2:25 pm CST and built rapidly to F2 strength. It survived for approximately 8 minutes, often returning briefly to a roped and tilted feature before it died. This tornado was followed by a second that formed near 2:35 pm CST. It built quickly into a multi-vortex tornado that appeared to be near F2 strength as well. This dissipated after only 4 minutes.

The final tornado from this same supercell, , the Jarrell Tornado, developed as a small...rope-shaped tornado, touching down around 2:40 pm CST inside the Williamson County line northwest of Jarrell. From film and eyewitness accounts, it expanded quickly into a very large vortex nearly 1/2 mile in width. Observations recounted by eyewitnesses indicated that the damage path may not have been made strictly by one tornado. A number of eyewitnesses reported seeing several small, rope-like funnels before the character of the tornado changed drastically into the killer tornado.

Ground damage patterns in the Double Creek Subdivision also suggested this possibility.

The tornado crossed CR 308, CR 305, and then CR 307. Where the tornado crossed each of these county roads, approximately 525 feet of asphalt was ripped off each of the roadways. This particular destruction was believed to be very close to the centerline of the tornado circulation. As the tornado crossed the intersection of CR 305 and 307, a business on the corner was destroyed. The tornado moved into the Double Creek area at this point with total destruction. F5 destruction continued from shortly after its formation until very close to the end of the damage path.

The tornado began a brief turn toward the southeast as it entered the Double Creek subdivision and the surrounding area, moving very slowly. It reached the subdivision at 3:48 pm. This time is based on a clock found at a destroyed residence in the extreme northwest corner of the subdivision and the home believed to be the first struck by the tornado. Here, it widened to it maximum width of three-quarters of a mile. From the air, the ground appearance changed abruptly in the vicinity of CR 308 and continued until very near the end of the path. No definitive circulation patterns or suction spots were evident, but there was the noted obvious change in the appearance of the ground. In the Double Creek area, approximately 40 structures were totally destroyed. One of the most striking signs in approaching this area was the distinct lack of debris of any size. Closer inspection showed lots of little debris but no sign of large items. It was estimated that several dozen vehicles had been in the subdivision and removed by the tornado. Nearly 300 cattle grazing in a pasture near the subdivision were also killed, with many of them tossed and blown for over 1/4 mile. At least half a dozen cars were identified from the air lying in the open areas, most of them flattened and encrusted with mud and grass. Trees in the subdivision were completely stripped of bark. Later ground survey revealed that most of the debris that was left in the area was extremely small indicating the power of the tornadic wind. All 27 deaths associated with the Jarrell tornado occurred in the Double Creek area. Eyewitnesses reported that it appeared to have slowed down as it entered the subdivision, and that may account for the nearly total destruction that took place.

After passing through the Double Creek area, the tornado shifted its track again slightly, moving toward the south-southwest across CR 309 and into a heavily wooded area of cedar trees. The total destruction of the tornado ends abruptly shortly after entering the wooded area. However, a small swath of tree damage on the north side of the main damage path suggested the possibility of a multiple vortex pattern. No other evidence of multiple vortices was observed.
The sequence of weather phenomenon reported with this tornado was exactly opposite of that often reported- the tornado first appeared, followed by nearly calm conditions, then hail, followed by rain and finally brief, gusty winds. This is attributed to the fact that the parent supercell was moving toward the southwest for most of its life. The storm essentially "backed into" the area as it moved.

From Storm Events Database, National Centers for Environmental Information, NOAA

Appendix C

The Victims of the Jarrell Tornado

Ruth Carmona (34)

Michael Carmona (15)

Satyn Carmona (13)

Bernice Gower (37)

Brian Gower (11)

Larry Igo (46)

Joan Igo (47)

Audrey Igo (17)

John Igo (15)

Paul Igo (15)

Katherine Parish Mayer (30)

Billy LaFrance (41)

Keith Moehring (40)

Cindy Moehring (40)

Erik Moehring (16)

Ryan Moehring (15)

Emma Mullins (44)

Ryan Fillmore (5)

Frederick Ripley (22)

Maria Ruiz (50)

John Ruiz (15)

Michael Ruiz (14)

Cindy Smith (36)

Brandi Smith (13)

Stacy Smith (10)

Vicki Taylor (36)

Jonathan Kehl (16)

Sources

<u>Personal Correspondence</u>

C. K. Boren, personal letter to author, May 2000.

Allen Meissner, personal letter to author, May 2000.

LaDonna Peterson, personal letter to author, May 2000.

Bruce Thomas, email to author, September 22, 2015.

<u>Newspapers</u>

> *Austin American Statesman*
> *Bryan/College Station Eagle*
> *Chicago Tribune*
> *Dallas Morning News*
> *LA Times*
> *Lewiston (ID) Tribune*
> *Temple Daily Telegram*
> *USA Today*
> *Wichita Eagle*

<u>Government publications</u>

Centers for Disease Control. "Tornado Disaster—Texas May 1997," *Morbidity and Mortality Weekly Report.* November 14, 1997.

Texas Department of Health. "Texas Tornado Disaster." *Disease Prevention News.* August 17, 1998.

U. S. Department of Commerce. National Oceanic and Atmospheric Administration. National Weather Service. *The Central Texas Tornadoes of May 27, 1997.* Silver Spring, Maryland, 1998.

U. S. Department of Commerce. National Institute of Standards and Technology. *The Fujita Tornado Intensity Scale: A Critique Based on Observations of the Jarrell Tornado of May 27, 1997.* Gaithersburg, Maryland, 1998.

Books and articles

Bradford, Marlene. *Scanning the Skies: A History of Tornado Forecasting.* Norman: University of Oklahoma Press, 2001.

Bradford, Marlene. *Texas Tornadoes: The Lone Star State's Deadliest Twisters.* Charleston: Marlene Bradford, 2016.

People Weekly. "Game Plan: Playing in Memory of Fallen Friends." Oct. 27, 1997, v48 n 17 p. 52.

Texas Co-op Power. "Twister." April 1999, v55 n10 p. 5.

Websites:

Aid Association for Lutherans. www.aal.org/AAL/about/news/Archive/1007/8-08-97.html.

Austin 360. www.austin360.com/news/05may/29/search.htm.

Sources

Baptist Press, Southern Baptist Convention. www.bpnnews.net/2389.

CNN Interactive. www.cnn.com/interactive/weather.

Find a Grave. www.findagrave.com.

KTVT CBS Dallas/Fort Worth. http://dfw.cbslocal.com

KXXV-TV Waco, Temple, Killeen. www.kxxv.com

My Fox Austin, "Jarrell ISD Installs Safe Rooms after 1997 Tornado." http://www.myfoxaustin.com

"May 27, 1997—the Jarrell, Texas Tornado."Stormstalker. https://stormstalker.wordpress.com/2012/11/23/jarrell/.

National Climatic Data Center. Storm Events Data Base. http://www.ncdc.noaa.gov/stormevents/eventdetails.

National Weather Service Fort Worth/Dallas. www.weather.gov/fwd.

National Weather Service Austin/San Antonio. www.weather.gov/ewx.

Portland Cement Association. www.cement.org.

Storm Prediction Center. www.spc.noaa.gov.

Stormtrack. "Foundation Survey at Jarrell, Texas." www.stormtrack.org/magazine/1997-11-v21-n1.pdf

WFAA ABC Dallas/Fort Worth. www.wfaa.com.

About the Author

Marlene Bradford has spent most of her life in Tornado Alley. When living in Lawrence, Kansas, Joe Eagleman, a meteorology professor at the University of Kansas, encouraged her to write tornado history. Her doctoral dissertation at Texas A&M University was the story of the tornado watch and warning system which was published under the title *Scanning the Skies: A History of Tornado Forecasting*. She is also the author of *Texas Tornadoes: The Lone Star State's Deadliest Twisters, Arkansas Tornadoes: The Natural State's Deadliest Twisters* and the editor of *Notable Natural Disasters*. Her love (besides tornadoes) is teaching. The author has recently retired from more than twenty years of teaching U.S. history at the college and high school level and currently resides with her husband in Garland, Texas.